Treasure hunting for all

a popular guide to a
profitable hobby

Treasure hunting for all

a popular guide to a
profitable hobby

by

Edward Fletcher

London
Blandford Press

First published 1973
by Blandford Press Ltd,
167 High Holborn, London WC1V 6PH
Reprinted 1975

© Edward Fletcher 1973

ISBN 0 7137 0645 7

Text set in 12 on 13 Bembo and
printed in Great Britain by
Unwin Brothers Limited
Old Woking, Surrey

Contents

Introduction   1

1 **Let's find some coins**   6
How to search a house to find lost coins

2 **Riverside treasure hunting**   14
Why rivers make such good sites—Historical notes—How to
construct simple tools for use on riversides—A look at three
typical sites

3 **Treasure hunting with a metal detector**   40
How detectors work—The best instrument for your needs—How
to find good sites—Coinshooting: how to succeed—Where to
find jewellery

4 **Treasure hunting on the coast**   67
Where to find coins on beaches—Sand sifting—Wintertime
treasure hunting—Wreck sites

5 **Hunting for hoards**   79
Why hoards are hidden—Some authentic stories—Hunting in
towns—Hunting in the countryside

6 **Treasure hunting problems**   89
A brief look at possible future developments in treasure hunting
equipment

7 **Bottles, pipes, and pot lids**   94
A brief look at dump digging

8 **Rockhounding**   102
Semi-precious gem hunting—Gold panning—Freshwater pearl
hunting

9 **Rules and regulations**   105
The amateur treasure hunters' Code of Conduct—The Treasure
Trove laws explained

10 **Useful addresses**   110
Clubs—magazines—suppliers of treasure hunting equipment

Index   112

Acknowledgements

The author and publishers are grateful to the following for their help in the preparation of this book: R. W. Collier and L. V. Pistone, who lent rock specimens; and Michael Allman, who took those photographs not supplied by the author.

Introduction

Here is a guide to Britain's fastest growing and most exciting hobby—treasure hunting. Whether a complete beginner or one of the many thousands of weekend enthusiasts who already enjoy the thrills of finding old coins, medals, badges, buttons, clay tobacco pipes, antique bottles, semi-precious stones, freshwater pearls, and other interesting and valuable collector's items, you will find much to interest you within its pages. There are chapters covering every problem the beginner might encounter—from buying basic equipment to finding profitable sites on which to hunt for amateur treasures—and many subjects of interest to old hands at the game have also been included. I am sure that all old hands will agree that a comprehensive book on the hobby is long overdue.

If anyone had suggested to me ten years ago that amateur treasure hunting might one day become a popular hobby for thousands of men, women, and children I would have shaken my head in disagreement. In those days I was one of a handful of eccentric lone wolves who made a tough living by digging Victorian rubbish dumps for old bottles,

Fig. I Children love treasure hunting. A riverside hunt produces many exciting finds and usually leads to a growing interest in local history.

jars, pot lids, and clay tobacco pipes which we sold to American collectors because there was no market on this side of the Atlantic. Occasionally we made trips into the wilder parts of Britain to pan for gold, hunt freshwater pearls, and search for semi-precious rocks and minerals. Equipment consisted of chest-length fishing waders, glass-bottomed buckets, river rakes, floating sieves, geological hammers, some rugged camping gear, and—in my case—a beaten-up van. The only sophisticated piece of gadgetry I owned was an ex Second World War mine detector. It was highly sensitive to hunks of old iron but failed, during the five years in which I lugged its fifteen pounds bulk weight over moor and mountain, to find a single object of value.

Some of my associates, frustrated at their lack of success with mine detectors, had turned to the underwater world of aqualungs and treasure wrecks in the hope of locating those elusive gold coins about which all of us dreamed. One or two were remarkably successful; but for most of us treasure hunting seemed likely to remain an unglamorous, unspectacular means of earning a living which held one great attraction: it was a life we loved.

Then, in the early 1960s, came the start of a series of events which were to make treasure hunting as a hobby possible for millions of people in the United States, Australia, and Great Britain. The first great leap towards universal popularity came when reliable electronic metal detectors, capable of locating small, non-ferrous objects such as coins and jewellery several inches under the ground, came onto the American market. They were expensive pieces of equipment and until 1965 sales were confined almost exclusively to the United States.

Next came the great mid-1960s boom in coin collecting which found most people in Britain searching the change in their pockets for rare pennies and halfcrowns worth a small fortune. The lucky few able to afford the one hundred and fifty pounds or more which it then cost to buy and import a reliable American metal detector found a ready market for every coin they could pull out of the ground. Within a year there were a few thousand detectors in use in Britain and this branch of the hobby became known by its American name of 'coinshooting'.

It did not take long for British electronics experts to see the potential for inexpensive metal detectors. Soon the first all-British model came on the market at under twenty pounds; by 1970 there were over a dozen models to chose from, and the number of weekend coinshooters in Britain had topped 30,000.

The collecting and polishing of semi-precious stones was another branch of the hobby to achieve wide popularity thanks to the introduction of inexpensive equipment. Thousands of weekend 'rockhounds' were soon combing the granite moors of Cornwall, the mountains of Wales, the Lake District, and the remoter parts of Scotland for amethyst, cairngorm, malachite, agate, and many other semi-precious stones which they shaped and polished in their home gem-cutting workshops to produce beautiful items of jewellery. By 1970 the number of British rock-hounds probably equalled the number of coinshooters—and the more enterprising were combining both as weekend pursuits.

Throughout the 1960s more and more people became interested in antique collecting, and all manner of Victoriana rocketed in price. Those who had taken to coinshooting were lucky. They could find their own collectors' items, or make a handsome profit by selling the badges, buttons, lead soldiers, tin whistles and other collectable metal objects they found. Those unable to afford the sky-high prices asked for conventional collectables looked around for something different, something interesting, something as yet untouched by the price spiral in the antique world. They found what they were looking for in bottles—the very bottles which the 1960s pioneers had been told would never be collected in Britain. At first only the well-known curiosities such as glass marble bottles and stone ginger beers were popular; but as more and more old bottles were recovered and interest in bottle history grew, the number of British 'bottle buffs' increased as rapidly as the number of coin-shooters and rockhounds had done during the previous decade. Thus coinshooting, rockhounding, and bottle collecting came to Britain—and those enthusiasts who enjoyed all three became known as amateur treasure hunters.

In the United States today amateur treasure hunting is one of the country's most popular hobbies. Geologically the country is a rockhound's paradise. Numerous semi-precious stones can be found in the mountains and deserts where ghost-towns remind one of the nineteenth-century mining booms when gold and silver worth millions of dollars was won from the igneous rocks in those regions. Now, a new 'gold rush' is underway. American bottle buffs and coinshooters have discovered the fortunes in bottles and relics which lie waiting in those old ghost towns, and amateur treasure hunters are heading for the hills once more to hunt coins, Americana, and other nineteenth-century relics in and around those boom towns of yesteryear.

An identical sequence of events is now leading Australia's large rockhounding fraternity back to the gold mining centres for which Australia was also famous when Queen Victoria sat on the throne of Britain. Already 20,000 Australian rockhounds have discovered that the old rubbish dumps on the outskirts of mining towns hold a fortune in Victorian bottles, pipes, and pot lids; already the first 'pioneer' coinshooters are at work and the truth that thousands of Victorian relics await the diligent searcher on these and many other Australian coinshooting sites is beginning to dawn. Soon others will follow and the great Australian coinshooting boom will get underway.

I hope that amateur treasure hunting enthusiasts in the United States, Australia, and elsewhere will read this book. The advice it gives on searching houses, open spaces, riversides, and beaches for coins, jewellery, and other collectables applies throughout the world and will lead all readers to exciting finds no matter where they live. The problems encountered when buying a metal detector, deciding where a miser might have hidden his fortune, locating those areas on a riverside where tides and currents will deposit coins—all are common to amateur treasure

4

hunters everywhere and all are covered within the pages of this book.

Are there *really* vast quantities of coins buried a few inches below the surface of the ground? *Is* it possible to build up a fine collection of military badges, antique buttons, or nineteenth-century jewellery with the aid of a metal detector? *Do* semi-precious gems await the diligent searcher who looks in the right places? *Can* Victorian pot lids be dug from long-forgotten rubbish dumps near almost any town or village? These are the questions which every experienced treasure hunter is asked by those who have yet to feel the thrill of a find. The answer is always YES; but the way in which that YES is delivered will vary with every treasure hunter you ask. Some, accustomed to the dis-belief of the uninitiated, will smile and nod and go their lonely ways. Others will show you a superb collection of coins or other historic relics and change the subject when you ask where and how they found them. I propose to answer your questions by asking you to read the following chapters of this book and then to put into practice the advice I have given. I guarantee that you will soon make exciting amateur treasure hunting finds if you do so.

Good hunting!

I Let's find some coins

150,000,000 coins disappear from circulation every year according to figures issued by the Central Statistics Office—and the majority are lost by careless people. If this figure surprises you ask yourself whether or not *you* have lost three coins during the past twelve months, and then consider that every other person in Britain has almost certainly done the same. All men know how easy it is to lose coins from trouser pockets while sitting in armchairs or deckchairs, or when lying on grassy slopes in parks or on commons; every woman knows how frequently change can slip from handbags and purses which are opened dozens of times in a day; and all youngsters know to their regret that small coins have a habit of slipping from clutching fingers when one is standing in a cinema queue or waiting to be served at an ice-cream van.

Such losses have happened for centuries. That is why professional coinshooters regularly find 30,000 coins in an average year, and why professional treasure hunters can confidently claim that there is sufficient money in the ground to pay off the National Debt and still leave enough to keep Britain's coinshooters busy for the rest of their lives. However, before we go on to discuss ways in which *you* can find your share of the wealth in the ground, I would like every reader to find one or two coins in his or her own home. This is the easiest way to make a start at amateur treasure hunting and I am confident that a number of readers will make quite valuable finds before they reach the end of this chapter.

Armchair losses   How much money would you estimate has passed through your house since it was first built? £10,000? £15,000? Well, let us take a house built in 1950 and estimate that the average income of the household from 1950 to the present (1973) has been £20 per week. No less than £23,000 will have passed through the pockets and purses of the people living there during those years. If we consider a house built in 1900 and reduce the average in-

come to only £10 per week the figure rises to well over
£36,000. Allowing only ten coins for every pound in
income (a very low figure when we consider the former
value of farthings and old pennies) would mean that at
least 360,000 coins have passed through the house since it
was first built. Small wonder that houses hold so many
valuable coin finds.

If you are reading this book while sitting in a comfortable
old armchair that has been hanging around your living room
for as long as anyone can remember you could be sitting
within a few inches of your first find. Remove the cushion
from the chair and slide your fingers gently between the
gap where the seat joins the arms and back. Press down-
wards on the seat as you do this and one or two coins or
other pocket losses should appear.

The next step is to search for those coins which have
managed to work their way through the gap to fall down
the arms or back and become trapped where the bottom
covering of the chair is fixed by nails or studs to the chair's

Fig. 2 Armchair losses.

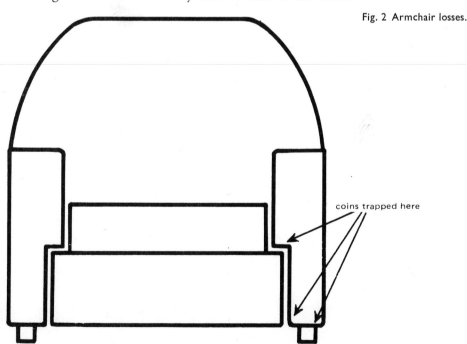

coins trapped here

7

wooden framework. If you pass your fingers very carefully along the bottom of the chair you will probably be able to feel the trapped coins through the outer covering. Do not turn the chair upside down in order to get at the coins. They will fall from their present position if you do so and probably become trapped in the springing. Support the chair so that two legs are off the ground and carefully remove the studs or nails with the aid of a pair of small pincers. Extract the coins and any other finds you make; replace the studs; then search the other side and the back in the same way. An average three-piece suite should hold ten coins—four in the settee and three in each chair—if it has not been searched by a previous owner. This means that in any small town with around 10,000 homes 100,000 coins are likely to have been lost by people simply taking the weight off their feet. It also means that if the face value of the coins in an average three-piece suite is as low as ten new pence, no less that £20,000 could be found in a city such as London.

Skirting board losses If you live in a house built in the nineteenth century— and there are millions of homes built when Queen Victoria sat on the throne—even more interesting finds can be made without leaving the house. Those readers who do not live in old houses are sure to have grandparents or other relatives living in houses built before 1900 who will be delighted at the prospect of their homes being searched by an amateur treasure hunter if you explain that your hunt for coins does not involve pulling their houses down around their necks. The only tool you will use for this particular search is a piece of stout wire about twelve inches long. Bend a two-inch hook at one end and your tool is ready for use.

Examine the skirting boards in the rooms of any house built at some time around the beginning of this century and you will find quite wide gaps between the skirting and the floor boards at various points around the walls. They are caused by sagging of supporting joists under the floor, and they occur most often in living rooms and hallways where lots of feet have tramped over the years and where heavy furniture has made its presence felt. Today fitted carpets usually cover these gaps, but at the beginning of this century such luxuries were almost unheard of. The average living-room floor or hallway had bare wooden floors which were stained, wax polished, and partly covered with rugs. In better-off homes the central area of the living-room floor might be covered by a square carpet; but few households could boast wall-to-wall floorcoverings, and in the larger properties several housemaids would have been kept fully employed waxing wide expanses of bare floor.

Vacuum cleaners were also unheard of. Those who did the housework were obliged to sweat with mops and heavy polishing buffs to keep the floors shining and this meant that any small coin carelessly dropped in the house was soon pushed under the gap in the skirting during cleaning operations. Thousands of these coins—rare date farthings, young head pennies, even the odd gold sovereign —can be found beneath the skirtings in old houses and the best spot to begin a search for those in your house is near front or back doors where numerous financial transactions such as paying the butcher, baker, and newspaper boy will have taken place over the years and where chances of coins being lost are very high.

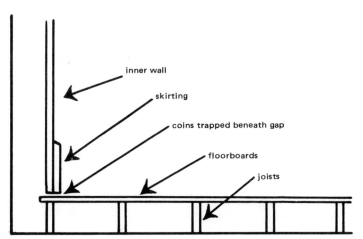

Fig. 3 Skirting board losses.

inner wall

skirting

coins trapped beneath gap

floorboards

joists

Check each skirting carefully to decide where gaps begin and end. Then take your bent wire and slide it carefully under the skirting at the start of the first gap. Make sure the wire remains flush with the floorboards as you draw it *slowly* along the gap and pull it gently towards you at the end of each run. Do not try to hurry the search. You may push valuable coins off the ends of the floorboards if you try to rush the job and this will make the task of recovering them much more difficult. Remember that any coins trapped here might have remained undiscovered for seventy or more years so there is no need to rush at this stage. Get into the habit of working slowly and methodically during these early amateur treasure hunting activities and you will soon learn that patience pays. Search all skirting board gaps very carefully in this way and you should end up with some interesting finds.

By this time one of the fundamental rules which amateur treasure hunters use to guide themselves to worthwhile sites should have begun to impress itself upon you: **Valuable finds are most likely to be made in those places where valuable losses are most likely to be made.** Appreciation of this simple rule is what distinguishes successful amateur treasure hunters from those people who persistently fail to make good finds. Every time you locate a collectable object you should ask yourself how and why it came to be in the place where you found it. Always, unless the object has been carried to the spot by a current, tide, or other natural force, the first part of the answer to that question will be: Because a human being lost, hid, or discarded the object there. Go on to discover what were the circumstances under which the object was lost, hidden, or discarded; find out what were the psychological and the physical reasons for that particular spot being chosen; and decide what that particular site has in common with others you will search in the future. When you begin to ask yourself these questions automatically whenever you make a find you will be moving towards a professional appreciation of treasure hunting.

But enough of theory for the present. Let us return to

the house and see if there are other places where coins are likely to have been lost. Try to imagine what it must have been like living in the house in Victorian times when a friendly coal fire in the living room was probably the focal point of family life. The mantelshelf above the fireplace would have been cluttered with many small personal possessions and it is almost certain that one or two items became lost when they fell into the gap usually found at the back of the mantelshelf where it joins the wall. Try a search there now with your bent wire.

Candles, paraffin lamps, and gas mantles provided lighting, but even in those houses equipped with gas life was somewhat gloomy after sunset. Substantial numbers of coins and other items were lost as people fumbled their way through dressing and undressing in poorly-lit bedrooms; numerous coins were lost as people tried to insert them into gas meters in total darkness; and very many small items which accidentally fell to the ground were lost forever. Remember that any coins you find inside the house are likely to be in excellent condition and should require only a gentle wash in warm soapy water to remove the greasy dust which will have covered and protected them over the years. You may only find a single, grubby-looking Victorian penny tucked away behind a disused gas meter or lying hidden beneath a bedroom skirting; but clean it up and it could turn out to be a penny minted in 1869. More than 2,500,000 of these coins were issued but if yours turns out to be one of the hundreds of specimens which must have been lost during the first few years after they were minted you could have a coin in very fine or even extremely fine condition—in which case your humble penny will be worth £45 to £70 (1973 values) and if you sell it you will have the purchase price of an excellent metal detector.

Children's losses

Knowledge of human behaviour is as important to a successful amateur treasure hunter as is knowledge of historical facts, figures, dates, and events. Concentrate on attempting to understand why people behave the way they

11

do and you will soon begin to understand why coins are always to be found in certain places. Fortunately for our purposes human nature has not changed significantly during the past 2,000 years. You can successfully improve your knowledge of how people behaved in the past by simply opening your eyes and observing your fellow human beings more closely. Victorian men, women, and children acted in very much the same way; so did the Romans; so will those people who colonize Mars in the next century.

Watch a small child at play in a house; give him a dozen coins and keep him under surreptitious observation during the next few days. You will be amused to see where he hides and loses his pennies, and his skill at finding little holes into which he can drop the coins will surprise you. I have lived in several houses during the past few years and I never cease to be amazed at the hiding places my daughter Karen, now aged four, finds for her 'little treasures'. Our previous home had a warm-air central heating system and the vents in floors and walls quickly became blocked with pennies, buttons, and small plastic objects from my daughter's toy box. In our present home an uneven kitchen floor has provided her with a safe deposit box under the fridge, while a doll who lost an arm in some unrecorded catastrophe has been converted to a makeshift money-box.

Victorian children did not have central heating vents into which coins could be dropped, but Victorian houses did have large, square locks fitted to the doors of every room and each lock had a wide and inviting keyhole which the majority of Victorian youngsters found irresistible as a hiding place for coins. If bedroom and kitchen doors in your house still have original locks you should make sure you search those locks at the first opportunity. Remove the screws which hold the body of the lock to the door and then carefully unscrew the backplate on the rear of the lock. Any coins or other small objects pushed into the keyhole in the past will have fallen to the bottom of the lock where they can, in fact, lie undisturbed for years because their presence does not interfere with the lock's mechanism. Extract any objects you find and the lock can then be replaced. Professional treasure hunters estimate that one lock in five holds objects of value, and the commonest lock finds are Victorian quarter, third, and half farthings which are usually in very fine condition.

Patience pays

I said at the beginning of this chapter that I wanted every reader to find one or two coins in his or her own home before we went on to consider finding objects buried in the ground. If you have carried out a methodical and painstaking search of furniture, skirting boards, and old locks in your property you should by now have succeeded in making your first find. If you have not yet done so I suspect that you have carried out your searches too quickly— a common mistake made by beginners. Go over the same areas once again very slowly; at the same time keep in mind the *second* fundamental rule for success at this hobby: **Patience pays.** Apply that rule now and you *will* succeed.

2 Riverside treasure hunting

Have you ever stood on an old bridge and looked down at the swirling water and wondered what might lie on the bed of the river flowing beneath your feet? Rare coins, beautiful jewellery, ancient weapons, perhaps even a long-lost treasure hoard? Such finds might seem highly improbable when you contemplate the bare pebbles, or dull and uninteresting mud of your local river; yet they represent only a small fraction of the countless historical, unusual, and valuable finds which have been made along riverbanks.

Visit your local museum and you will see on display many objects which have been picked up on riversides by men, women, and children working or playing near rivers in every county in Britain. Flint axe-heads, bone tools, bronze shields, iron spears, Roman coins, Anglo-Saxon brooches, Medieval pottery, Victorian pistols, a chest containing 20,000 silver pennies, even a complete ship more than one thousand years old. The list is endless; the variety of objects found quite astonishing.

In this chapter I will explain how you can join in this historical riverside treasure hunt and find objects similar to those mentioned above. You may not locate a vast hoard of treasure, but if you set about the project in the correct way, learn something of the history of your local river, and the way in which river currents move and deposit objects along riversides, you are certain of some exciting finds. Some of the tools required for riverside treasure hunting can be made quite easily from everyday objects, while more sophisticated equipment such as suction dredges and water-immersible metal detectors are obtainable from several suppliers. However, the success of the project really depends on your own powers of observation and on knowing as much as possible about the sort of finds you might come upon, and how and why they found their way into the water.

Rivers and history Ever since men first discovered they could float on water by sitting astride a fallen log, rivers have been used for transport and as a source of food. The earliest man-made objects lost in rivers were probably flint arrowheads and bone fish-hooks used by Stone Age hunters who wandered across Britain more than 5,000 years ago; the most recent are probably the new halfpennies which many foreign visitors to London throw into the Thames from West-minster Bridge. During those 5,000 years between the Stone Age and the Tourist Age millions of objects have joined the arrowheads and fish-hooks and rivers have played a vital role in our wars, our communications, and our commercial growth.

Even before the arrival of William the Conqueror, earlier settlers had used our waterways as trade routes. Bronze Age metal workers established a sea and river trade network which linked the gold of Ireland with the gold buyers of the Continent. The Romans built bridges, paved fords, and even cut canals; while the Danes established thriving ports on a number of rivers and laid down the foundations for Britain's later maritime successes. But it was not until after the arrival of the Normans that the vigorous growth of cities, ports, and trade really got underway.

It was along the rivers that medieval kings, barons, and bishops transported huge blocks of stone to build their fortresses, cathedrals, bridges, and abbeys; and it was those towns sited close to navigable rivers which grew to pro-minence. By the end of the thirteenth century some eight million sheep fleeces were being loaded every year at these ports for export to the Continent. The vessels which carried them returned laden with French wines, Spanish leather, and Portuguese oranges and lemons. Lead tallies, used to identify bales of wool, and merchants' tokens, used when small coins were scarce, often turn up around the wharves of these medieval ports; as do the tools of the tradesmen who lived and worked in these great commercial centres.

Wars continued, of course, and large numbers of medieval weapons have turned up in rivers, often close to fords and bridges which now became important strategic points. Arrowheads and crossbow bolts are the commonest finds, though pikes and cannonballs have also turned up. A spectacular war chest is included in the riverside finds dating from the Middle Ages. It was found near a bridge not far from Burton-on-Trent and it contained 20,000 silver pennies lost by the Earl of Lancaster when he tried to cross the river during a flood.

Merchant ships increased in size throughout the Middle Ages and ports nearer to the sea, where large vessels could be berthed, grew in importance. The inland riverside towns were increasingly served by barges which carried goods to and from the estuary ports where wharves, cranes, and warehouses were built. In this way Newcastle-upon-Tyne prospered as the estuary port for coal, corn, lead, leather, and wool shipped down the Tyne from smaller Northumberland towns. Hull, which in Anglo-Saxon times was a small fishing village, began to attract vessels which had previously unloaded their cargoes at Beverley or York. Boston, linked by the Witham to Lincoln, became the main centre for the handling of Lincolnshire wool, and Lynn handled the exports and imports of the abbeys at Ely, Ramsey, and Crowland. Yarmouth overtook Norwich as the main port in Norfolk, and Ipswich rose to prominence as the main centre for the export of Suffolk cheese and bacon. On the south coast Southampton became the seaport for wool arriving by barge from the rivers of Hampshire and Wiltshire, while Bristol became the meeting point for barges coming down the Severn and merchant ships arriving from Spain and Portugal.

Most spectacular of all was the growth of medieval London. A description of the city written during these times records that two thousand small boats and a great number of huge barges carried passengers, provisions, and exports from all quarters of Oxfordshire, Berkshire, Buckinghamshire, Hertfordshire, Middlesex, Essex, Surrey, and Kent into the port. Other rivers including the Severn, the Ouse, and the Trent were equally busy and today their tidal foreshores abound with interesting objects lost or thrown into the water. Medieval coins, pewter mugs, brass candlesticks, a wide variety of pottery and ship's fittings, together with many items from foreign vessels have all turned up on such sites.

In the late Middle Ages exports of raw wool declined rapidly as more and more cloth was produced in this country. This increased the number and variety of foreign vessels visiting Britain to load English cloth which soon achieved world-wide fame for its quality. There was a similar increase in the number of barges moving up and down the inland rivers to collect this new export from the many watermills which were now built to process the raw wool into cloth.

Overland traffic also increased in medieval times and some of the old Roman roads came into use again as cart tracks. Teams of horses carried wool, cloth, corn, lead, and other products from the highland areas to the nearest riverside town which was served by barges. This resulted in the building of many pack horse bridges over mountain streams. Unlike the larger town or city bridges they did not have religious shrines at their centres where monks sold medallions and badges to pay for the upkeep of the bridge. Nevertheless, these small countryside bridges make first-class sites for river and stream hunting because they were frequently the scenes of unfortunate accidents when mountain streams were in flood. Many cargoes and not a few men and horses were lost in wintertime crossings when streams suddenly became raging torrents. Ferries and fords were also much used in these areas and their sites also produce many worthwhile finds including horseshoes, horse brasses, boat fittings, and coins used to pay the ferryman for his services.

After 1600 Britain began to rely less on agriculture and more on manufactured goods for her wealth. Industry and population grew rapidly, and soon the pack horse teams and existing river routes proved inadequate for the massive movements of raw materials and finished goods which became increasingly important. The first improvements were made by increasing the navigable lengths of many rivers. This was done by dredging and it brought to many towns relying on slow and expensive pack horse teams a quicker and less costly river barge service. The next step was to provide 'cuts' between river bends, or meanders, so that river routes from town to town became more direct and a speedier collection and delivery service could be offered. By 1700 these improvements had provided Britain with over 1,000 miles of usable waterway. The Severn could carry barge traffic for 180 miles to Welshpool in Montgomeryshire; the Wye connected Hay, a town 100 miles inland, with the Bristol Channel; and quite large vessels could reach Oxford on the Thames. Towns such as Nottingham, Shrewsbury, Stratford-on-Avon, Peterborough, Hertford, Bedford, and Cambridge were all large inland ports at this time.

Yet even this excellent river system proved insufficient for the industrial expansion which took place during the next century. Raw materials such as coal, iron ore, and pottery clay were required by new industries which often grew up in areas where there were no large rivers which barges could use. To carry such heavy materials by pack horse or cart was uneconomical and the the only answer lay in providing man-made canals. Between 1750 and 1850 canals were built to link every major town and industry with a seaport. The entire system spanned the country and even managed, by the use of locks, to carry waterways over mountains. The total length of the system, including rivers and canals, was almost 5,000 miles when it reached its peak in 1850. Today, largely because of competition from railways and modern roads, only 2,000 miles of the system are in use. Nevertheless, very long journeys can still be made by river craft. It is possible to travel from London to York along an excellent river and canal route now used by both industrial barges and holiday-makers enjoying the delights of inland cruising.

Many of the old canals make first-class treasure hunting sites, particularly around disused lock gates and along the almost dry meanders which fell out of use when 'cuts' were introduced. Look out for some of the beautiful brass fittings from old barges, and the richly decorated crockery which canal folk used.

The American Colonies and the British Empire introduced many new products to these islands from the sixteenth century onwards. One which has left perhaps the greatest legacy of riverside finds is tobacco. From Tudor times until the beginning of the twentieth century tobacco was smoked in clay pipes. Thousands of them were thrown into rivers by seamen and bargees when their fragile stems were broken by an unfortunate blow. Many of the pipe bowls were delightfully decorated and they are well worth finding because the stems can be repaired quite easily.

The variety of foreign coins, jewellery, and other items lost in Britain's rivers also increased enormously after 1600. Seamen from every nation visited our river estuaries and most of them left us some small object lost or thrown into the river to remind us of their visit. British seamen returning from foreign ports still have the habit of throwing small coins picked up in distant ports into the river as they leave the ship. Blackfriars foreshore on the Thames has a rich scattering of Chinese coins dating from the eighteenth and nineteenth centuries when wharves in that area were used by vessels with Chinese crews, and many early American coins have been found alongside Mersey and Southampton docking areas. Large amounts of Victorian coinage and jewellery also found their way into rivers in Victorian times by way of town and city drainage systems which all flowed into rivers.

Another practice which became very common in Victorian times was that of building up river banks to prevent flooding, to reclaim land, and to increase the depth of water in rivers. The material used to strengthen banks very often contained large amounts of household rubbish. This has resulted in many items from the nineteenth century finding their way into the water because of river-bank erosion. Metal buttons, military badges, pins, pottery, cutlery, and many Victorian bottles are among the items you can expect to find along the embanked stretches of such rivers.

And so to the present day when history, as always, continues to repeat itself. The number of low denomination modern coins which have found their way into rivers since the introduction of decimal coinage is staggering. Many professional treasure hunters are of the opinion that the number of halfpennies which are being lost or thrown away will shortly become so high that the Royal Mint will find the cost of replacing them prohibitive. I wonder how many readers have themselves thrown a half-penny from a bridge into a river during the past twelve months? Keep it up! You are adding to the storehouse of finds which will be made by treasure hunters in the future.

This fleeting survey of river history will have given you some idea of the finds to be made along riversides. It may also have suggested possible hunting grounds along your local waterside. The next step is to visit your local library and read all you can about the history of your city, town, or village and its local port, river, or canal. Such research will soon reveal the locations of old fords, ferries, bridges, moorings, and docking areas where you can be sure of finding some of the items mentioned above.

Basic tools Readers of my earlier books, *Bottle Collecting* and *Rock and Gem Polishing* will know the value of glass-bottomed buckets and plastic tubes when used to search rivers and streams for bottles and semi-precious gems. These two items of equipment are equally useful when searching shallow water for coins, jewellery, and other small valuables. Make the bucket by removing the bottom from a metal waste paper bin and securing a piece of glass over the hole with waterproof adhesive. The tube, which is used to search deeper water, is made by gluing a piece of glass over the end of a three-foot length of p.v.c. soil pipe.

A river rake serves four purposes. Firstly, it is used to draw towards you objects which lie on the riverbed in water too deep to wade in. Secondly, it is used to pick up your finds from the riverbed without wetting the sleeves of your coat. Thirdly, it is designed in such a way that even small objects such as coins can be picked up quite easily. Fourthly, it enables you to work in safety in the water.

To make the rake you will require:

Two pieces of three-quarter inch marine ply (9in. ×
4in.)
Broom handle
Strip of half-inch wire netting (20in. × 4in.)
Hand or electric drill with two bits (5·16in. and
3·16in.)
16 six-inch nails
4 two-inch coach bolts with nuts (5·16in.)
2 four-inch coach bolts with nuts (5·16in.)
Fine copper wire
Spanner to fit coach bolt nuts.

Take two pieces of three-quarter inch marine ply
measuring nine inches by four inches and place them one
on top of the other. You must now drill two holes passing
through both pieces of wood which will be used to bolt
the handle of the rake to the head. These holes are made
in the centre of the wood (four and a half inches from each
end) and should be drilled approximately one inch from
the edges. Make them five-sixteenths of an inch in diameter.
Four more holes must be drilled through both pieces of
wood at this stage. They are positioned one inch from each
corner and, again, should be five-sixteenths of an inch in
diameter (see Fig. 4a).

Having drilled all six holes, set aside one piece of wood
and draw a pencil line down the nine-inch length of the
other piece. This line should pass down the middle of the
wood (two inches from either side) and is used as a guide
line when drilling the holes for the tines (prongs) of the
fork. These holes, which should all be three-sixteenths of
an inch in diameter, are now drilled at half-inch centres
down the pencil line. Make the first hole half an inch from
one end and you should finish up with a line of sixteen
holes (see Fig. 4b).

Into these holes you must now carefully hammer the
six-inch nails. As each nail is driven home bend it slightly
towards one edge of the plywood so that all the nails are
angled towards you. Now take the other piece of plywood

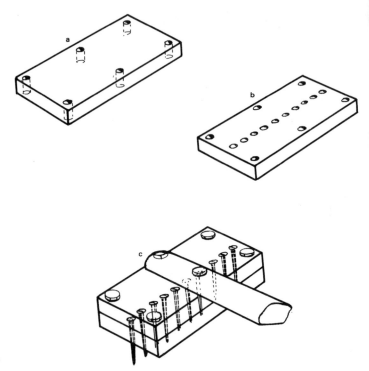

Fig. 4 River rake details.

and place it over the nail heads. Using two-inch coach bolts passed through the corner holes in both pieces of wood, tighten the nuts with a spanner so that the nail heads are sandwiched between the pieces of plywood. This will prevent the nails working loose when you dig the tines into the riverbed.

Now take a broom handle and mark on one end the positions of the two remaining holes in the plywood and drill two five-sixteenth-inch holes in the handle at the points indicated. You can now secure the shaft by passing two four-inch bolts through the broom handle and both pieces of plywood. Tighten the nuts firmly with a spanner.

Finally, take a piece of half-inch wire netting four inches wide and twenty inches long and weave it through the nails; first from one end, then the other. Its purpose is to act as a trap for very small objects which might slip between

22

Fig. 5 Test the riverbed with your rake before you enter the water.

the tines. Secure it to the nails at each end of the head with fine copper wire (see Fig. 4c).

The other tool which you should make for yourself is a floating sieve which is used to wash gravel and mud dug from exposed riverbanks to extract possible finds. Make it by placing a garden sieve in the centre of an inflated inner tube from a car tyre. Secure it to the tube with plastic coated wire at four points around its circumference. An anchor weight should be tied to a length of plastic wire and secured to the bottom of the sieve. This will prevent the sieve floating off downstream when in use. Incidentally, it is wise to carry an inner tube repair outfit and a foot pump when visiting remote sites.

In addition to the equipment mentioned above you will also need a pair of long wellingtons, a lightweight spade, a garden trowel, and some plastic bags for your finds.

23

Safety   Riverside treasure hunting is no more dangerous than any other outdoor hobby—**if** the rules of the game are carefully observed. Those rules are:

1. Never walk into the river before you have tested the bed with your river rake.
2. Never walk in the water parallel with the bank.
3. Always enter and leave the water by the same route.
4. Never venture into deep water. All the finds are to be made close to the banks.
5. Think before you act.

Stick to those safety rules and I guarantee enjoyment and lots of finds. Break them and you will ruin the project and probably go home empty-handed.

Eddy currents   At the beginning of this chapter I asked if you had ever stood on an old bridge and wondered what might lie on the bed of the river beneath your feet. You now know that such a site might hold weapons, tools, coins, jewellery, pottery, glassware, clay tobacco pipes, badges, medallions, and many other items of value. I would now like to explain how it is possible to locate those spots in the river which are most likely to hold some of those objects. It does not matter whether the location is a bridge, a ford, a disused canal, or a tidal river estuary; the way in which objects are moved and deposited on a riverbed is the same on any and every stretch of running water.

Let us suppose that the site you have chosen is a bridge over a non-tidal stretch of river. Look downstream from the bridge; watch the surface of the water carefully, and observe that although the river is flowing generally in one direction there are swirls of water which seem to move in great circles below the bridge supports. You will also see that the water in the middle of the river flows much faster than the water near the banks. In some places, particularly the sheltered areas around the supports, the water hardly seems to flow at all.

These differences in speed and direction occur on every river. They are the results of eddy currents which are

caused by obstructions to the general flow of the river. The obstruction might, as in this case, be a bridge support; it could also be a sudden change in the direction of the river, a submerged rock, a bump in the riverbed, a landing stage, a stone wall, or a man-made bank which narrows the channel through which the river flows. Whatever the obstruction, its effect is to cause eddy currents and to make the river alter its course and its speed.

You should make a sketch of the river as you see it from the bridge and mark on it those areas where the swirls and the slower-moving stretches of water occur. Indicate the positions of one or two objects on the river banks—a house or some trees—so that when you are down on the riverside, where it is more difficult to see the eddy swirls,

Fig. 6 Eddy currents. Note the area of slow-moving water on the left of the picture.

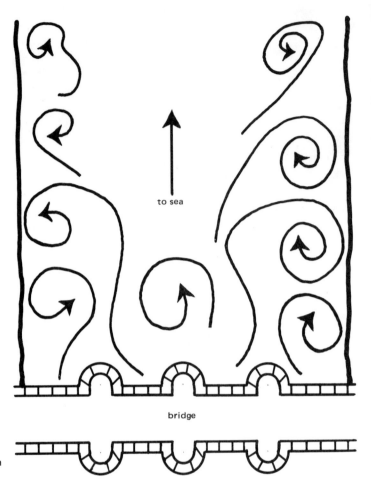

to sea

bridge

Fig. 7 Eddy currents seen
from bridge.

you will be able to locate those spots by reference to objects
on the banks.

**Speed and
movement**
Fast flowing water is able to move much heavier objects
than water which is flowing slowly. This may seem obvious,
but you will probably be surprised to learn that if the
speed of the flow is doubled, the water's power to move
objects is increased sixty-four times.

What would happen to a coin thrown from the bridge
we have been discussing? If the river ran absolutely straight,
if its bed was absolutely level, and if there were no obstruc-

tions to the flow, the coin would be moved gradually along the bed of the river until it reached the sea. But the river is not straight and there are, as we have seen, many obstructions which cause the water to flow in different directions. The coin would be caught by an eddy current and swept along the bottom in a wide, circular movement which would carry it towards one of the banks until it reached a point where the speed of the current could no longer move it. Here it would come to rest. This is what has happened to every object dropped or thrown from the bridge since it was first built.

The side of the river you look at first should be that which your historical research shows to have been most used by people in the past. This will usually be the side where access to the water is easiest—with steps, a landing stage, or even a tow path to help you get down to the

Searching in the water

Fig. 8 Using the glass-bottomed bucket to search the riverbed.

river. At the water's edge you should walk fifty yards downstream from the bridge before entering the water so that silt is carried away by the current as you work upstream towards the bridge. Remembering the safety rules, test the bottom with your rake. If the bed is firm step into the water by placing your feet on the spot you have just tested; if the bed is too soft, return to the bank, move a yard or so upstream, and test with the rake once more.

When you get into the water allow the silt to settle and then look carefully at the bed through your glass-bottomed bucket. There are two things you must look for initially— areas of fine sand or mud, and areas of shingle or pebbles less than two inches in diameter. Fine sand or mud downstream from the bridge will not hold metal objects because they would have been dropped *before* the current lost its power to carry fine sand. On the other hand, spots in the river downstream from the bridge where the current dropped pebbles will also be the spots where metal objects of similar weight to the pebbles were dropped. Take an even closer look at the bed here and you will probably see small pieces of metal or broken glass mixed with the pebbles or shingle. If you see any washers or pieces of copper or lead then you have found a spot which is almost certain to hold coins, metal buttons, and possibly items of jewellery.

Weight distribution The lesson to be learned from a survey of the riverbed through a glass-bottomed bucket is that in rivers objects are generally distributed by the currents according to their weight. It is a rule which applies to every river in the world, and one which the gold prospectors in North America, Australia, and Africa have put to use many times. Gold, being a very heavy metal, is dropped even by the powerful currents in mountain streams very soon after it enters the water. To find the source of the gold, or Mother Lode as it is known, a prospector works his way upstream with his gold pan. As he gets closer to the Mother Lode the tiny flakes of gold which he pans from the gravel in the bed become gradually larger. Close to the original source he may be lucky and find half-inch nuggets trapped

in a crevice on the bed. Such a spot is known as a 'glory hole' and when a prospector finds one he knows that the rich gold vein of the Mother Lode is in the rocks somewhere nearby.

Returning to our bridge, your search should be concentrated on those areas where a pebble or shingle bottom is revealed. There may be half a dozen such areas between the point at which you start your search and the bridge towards which you should work. Do not walk in the water when trying to find them. Leave the water after each survey with your bucket and move a yard or two nearer the bridge. If you do this you will not run the risk of stepping into any deep holes in the bed.

Fig. 9 Raking the riverbed after the first survey through the glass-bottomed bucket.

When searching each area of pebbles you should look first for interesting objects which might be visible immediately. Do not expect to see shining discs of copper, silver, or gold; nor a gleaming sword or highly polished antique pistol. All metal objects will appear a greenish black colour because the river applies a camouflaging coat to every object which rests on its bed. Look instead for particular shapes—round, square, oblong, anything which looks unlike a pebble. You may pick up lots of junk at first, but if you are patient it will not be long before you make a worthwhile find. Use your river rake to lift objects off the bottom. Draw the object towards you with the tines until it is close to your feet; dig the tines into the bed behind the object and lift the head of the rake vertically out of the water. The wire mesh will trap even the smallest object.

After picking up all the objects which you see through the bottom of the bucket you should rake the area thoroughly, allow the silt to settle, and examine the bed once again for objects which the rake has uncovered. Use this search method on each patch of shingle or pebbles you find as you work towards the bridge. If you mark the location of each find you make on the sketch you drew when standing on the bridge you will see that the eddy currents correspond with the most productive areas of the riverbed.

Tidal riversides   There are approximately three hundred tidal rivers around the coast of Britain and a treasure hunt along any one of them cannot fail to produce interesting finds. All the rules about eddy currents and dropping points which aid your search on inland rivers apply equally to tidal riversides; but here you have the additional advantage of a rising and falling tide. When the tide goes out you can walk dry-shod along the exposed foreshore and pick up many valuable objects. You can also see and examine at close quarters the bumps, depressions, river walls, landing stages, rocks, bridge supports, and other obstacles which cause eddy currents. For this reason alone a visit to a tidal riverside is worth the effort; it will teach you much about currents on inland rivers and will greatly improve your chances of making good finds on every waterway.

It is important when visiting a tidal site to know the times of high and low water on the day of your visit. This information can be obtained from the offices of the local River Authority from where you will also be able to purchase a copy of the yearly tide tables. These tables are particularly useful if you plan to make regular trips to the tidal reaches of that river because they will give you the times of high and low water at a number of points along the river on every day of the year. They will also tell you when to expect the highest and lowest levels of water from which you can work out the area of foreshore which will be exposed on any particular day.

Let us suppose you have chosen another bridge site on your tidal river. You may have selected the spot because the modern bridge stands on the site of an earlier bridge or ford; your historical research has perhaps revealed that the banks on both sides of the bridge were important mooring and docking areas two or three hundred years ago; or the river itself may have been a busy thoroughfare for several centuries. Whatever the reason for your choice, the bridge makes an ideal spot from which to look at the river before going down to the water's edge. Try to arrive just as the high tide begins to turn and you will have several hours in which to follow the river down to its low water mark before the tide turns again. Look downstream from the bridge and make a sketch of the river, marking on it all eddy currents, landing stages, walls, steps, nearby buildings, or trees, and decide on the best access to the water's edge.

As the tide begins to fall, you may see small 'islands' of dry foreshore several yards from the water's edge. These are the high spots on the riverbed and they should correspond with some of the eddy currents you marked on your sketch at high tide. They are the most important search areas on any tidal river and their exact locations should be carefully noted. You should also look for submerged walls or

Fig. 10 Sketches made from bridge.

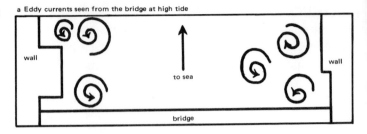

a Eddy currents seen from the bridge at high tide

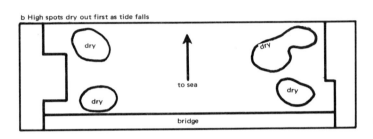

b High spots dry out first as tide falls

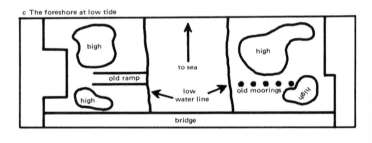

c The foreshore at low tide

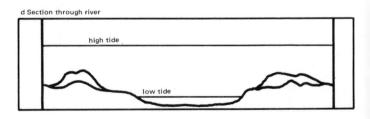

d Section through river

old timber piles which are revealed as the water goes down. They can trap objects moving along the river bottom and they are always worth close investigation. When the water has receded far enough to give access to your selected search area make your way down to the riverside. Bear in mind that steps and walls which have been underwater will be slippery and perhaps covered with moss, or even seaweed on sites near the river mouth. Walk on them with care.

First impressions on a tidal foreshore are usually of a great muddle of rocks, masonry, driftwood, scrap metal, pebbles, and mud; but if you look closely you will see that there is some order in the way objects are scattered across the banks. Large stones and pieces of heavy masonry will almost certainly be at the top of the foreshore, and most of the larger pieces of metal will lie quite close together at certain points. Consult your sketch and locate one of the high spots you saw from the bridge by reference to nearby

Fig. 11 Your eyes are your most useful tool on a tidal foreshore. Search interesting spots slowly and carefully.

33

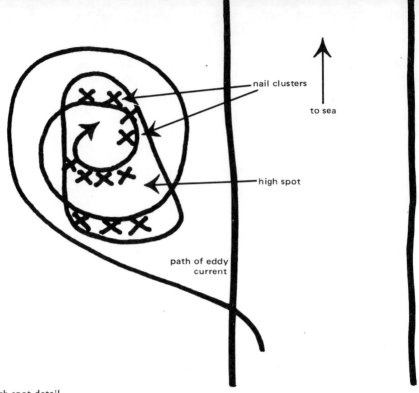

nail clusters

to sea

high spot

path of eddy
current

Fig. 12 High spot detail.

steps, buildings, or trees. It will not be as high or as raised
from the general level of the foreshore as you expected it
to be because it takes only a very slight unevenness on
the riverbed to set up an eddy current.

Use your eyes most carefully at this point; squat down
to bring the surface as close as possible and scan every inch.
You will soon begin to find copper nails, pins, and small
pieces of lead lying in neat clusters around the high spot.
They were dropped at these points because the current lost
some of its power after whirlpooling around the raised
area and could no longer carry these heavier items. Somewhere within those clusters you should begin to find the
'treasures' of tidal riversides—coins, rings, brass buttons,
military badges, bracelets, old keys, lead fishing weights,
Victorian toys, clay tobacco pipes, musket balls, and many
other finds. You will not see them immediately, but if you
concentrate on picking up all symmetrically shaped objects
such as washers, nails, and screws, you will soon make a
good find. When the entire high spot has been searched in

34

Fig. 13 Rake the area thoroughly after your first search. This will turn up other finds lying just below the surface.

this way comb the surface with your river rake to turn pebbles, gravel, and metal clusters to expose those finds lying just beneath the surface.

Consult your sketch and select a spot with an eddy current which has not yet been uncovered by the falling tide. When the river is sufficiently shallow to wade in at this spot your floating sieve—with its anchor weight securely attached—should be placed in the water. Position your hands on the top of the inner tube and press up and down. This will cause water to rise and fall through the bottom of the sieve. Now rake into heaps the loose pebbles, gravel, and odd pieces of metal which are exposed as the river level slowly falls. The washing action caused by the up-and-down movement of the sieve floats away all mud, silt, and small pebbles and leaves in the bottom of the sieve those objects too large to pass through the holes. Valuable finds can then be removed before the sieve is emptied by turning it upside down. Do not overload the sieve. Two or three spadefuls of unwashed material should

Using the floating sieve

Fig. 14 Loading the sieve.
Do not over-fill.

be dealt with each time, and the sieve then cleaned out before new material is added. You must also move down the foreshore as the river level falls to ensure that there is at least six inches of water below the sieve at all times.

Traps   Any old walls or wooden piles exposed at low tide also merit attention, particularly if they lie at right angles to the flow of the river. Valuable objects are often trapped on the upstream side of such obstacles. To search a trap thoroughly first rake out the pebbles, shingle, and mud which have collected at the base on the upstream side to a depth of six inches. Spread them evenly across the riverside and go over the material very carefully with your eyes. Pick up any objects which attract your immediate attention and then use your glass-bottomed bucket to carry

36

water to the spot. Pour several buckets of water over the material to wash away the mud and silt and then search the residue once again.

Recording your finds

You should cultivate the habit of recording finds you make on every site you visit because such records are most helpful when seeking new amateur treasure hunting locations. Your research will often indicate likely spots which have a similar layout to those already visited; if you can refer back to a detailed record showing where the best finds were made on previous sites you will be more than halfway to finding those on your new sites. Mark the location and a brief description of each find on your sketch as you search the area. The sketch can then be used to start a file of site records which will prove invaluable for future research.

Leaving the riverside

Remember that the tide comes in just as surely as it goes out. Always keep an eye on the river when working tidal sites and allow sufficient time to leave the area safely. As the tide begins to rise spend a few minutes raking over the areas which you have searched during the visit. Level all heaps of pebbles or gravel you have made and tidy the site to leave it as you found it. There is a bonus to be gained by raking the site in this way. During the high tides between

Fig. 15 (*left*) Wash away all mud, sand, and other loose material.

Fig. 16 (*right*) Sift out the interesting finds.

this search and your next visit the currents will move and grade the loose material once again. This will uncover new finds to await your next treasure hunt on that particular stretch of foreshore.

River meanders   Let us now take a brief look at another typical site—a shallow, fast-flowing stream in hilly countryside which has a small bridge by which a narrow road crosses the water. If the site is a ford which has been paved or which has stepping stones beneath the water you should search the upstream side of these obstructions carefully. If the site is bridged the supports, however small, will set up eddy currents. They will be difficult to see because of the numerous small currents caused by rocks and boulders in the stream but if you use your glass-bottomed bucket to search the stream sides you will soon locate those areas where smaller material has been dropped. Use your rake to turn the pebbles and you may find coins and other interesting items lying beneath them.

The spot you *must* locate near such a site is the first bend in the course of the stream below the ford or bridge. Such bends, or meanders, make interesting sites on all streams and rivers. On the inner bend of every meander you will find an area where small objects are always deposited by currents. When the mass of water pouring downstream strikes the bank on the outer bend it is swung from its path towards the opposite bank. This causes a

Fig. 17 A meander.

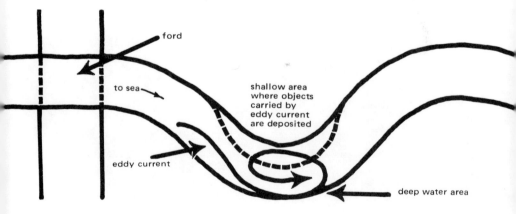

ford

to sea

shallow area
where objects
carried by
eddy current
are deposited

eddy current

deep water area

38

great eddy current which swirls across the stream to the inner bend. Here it loses momentum and drops heavier objects which are certain to include many from the ford or bridge further upstream.

When walking from the bridge or ford to the first bend make sure you are on the bank which will bring you to the *inside* of the meander. The water is usually quite shallow on such sites and you will be able to search a wide area of the inner bend with your glass-bottomed bucket and river rake. The outer bend will always be deep because large amounts of material from the bottom will have been carried across the stream to the opposite bank. If you were to throw a coin into the deep water on the outer bend it would, in time, be carried by the eddy current to the shallows on the inner bend.

There are thousands of sites like those discussed in this chapter on rivers, canals, and streams everywhere. All have two common factors: They are sites which were used by large numbers of people in the past; and they are sites where eddy currents in the water cause the objects which you hope to find to be deposited at certain points along the riverbed. If you look for those two characteristics—the first in your historical research, the second in your search on the sites you select—you will have similar success on any riverside location.

Finding new sites

3 Treasure hunting with a metal detector

There is no doubt that the rise in popularity of amateur treasure hunting as a hobby is directly linked to the availability of inexpensive metal detectors. The idea of using a lightweight electronic 'box-of-tricks' to locate valuables lost or hidden beneath the surface of the ground captures the imagination of most people with a spark of adventure flickering in their bones. We have all read *Treasure Island*; we all catch gold fever as readily as we catch a cold; and the urge to rush out and buy a detector the moment we learn that they can indeed quite readily be purchased is hard to resist.

Be warned, however, that suppliers of treasure hunting equipment do not sell magic wands which will guide you by electronic extra-sensory perception to a chest of Spanish gold. A metal detector is a tool—just one of several—in a treasure hunter's equipment bag, and like all tools it must be used intelligently and correctly if it is to do the job for which it was designed. You would not expect to become an experienced soccer player by purchasing a pair of football boots; you would not challenge the club pro to a match the day after buying your first set of golf clubs. Only practice, time, and patience can bring success at those activities—and they are equally important when treasure hunting with a metal detector.

Having dampened your spark of adventure somewhat, let me add that you should be able to find half a dozen modern coins within half an hour of buying your first unit. If you apply the rules set out in this chapter diligently and patiently you should, within a few weeks, be able to find fifty or more coins and several items of jewellery during a full day spent coinshooting on footpaths, beaches, riversides, and commons. Make a professional study of the subject and your rewards from coinshooting will total several hundred pounds per year; while your chances of a really big find will be greatly increased. Hoards of considerable value have been found by enthusiastic amateur treasure hunters in recent years and many more await discovery. Whether or not you make a major find, you will certainly reap a substantial reward in pleasure, in knowledge, and in relaxation if you use your metal detector in the way it should be used—as a useful tool and an electronic aid to assist you in the enjoyment of your hunt.

In Britain the first widely publicized Treasure Trove find located with a metal detector (The Grove Wood Treasure) was discovered by an amateur treasure hunter using one of the least expensive detectors available at that time. The unit cost £12·50 and it earned for its owner a reward of several thousand pounds.

Which detector should you buy

At the opposite end of the scale is a professional treasure hunter who specializes in coinshooting. He uses one of the most expensive and sophisticated detectors on the market and he finds up to 30,000 coins, rings, badges, antique buttons, buckles, medals, keys, and brooches in an average year. Many of the coins he finds have only face value; others are worth as much as £50 each, and he can confidently expect to find at least one minor hoard during a period of twelve months.

Between these two extremes—the simple detector used by the amateur mentioned above (who, incidentally, has now progressed to a serious interest in treasure hunting) and the expensive unit used by the professional—lies a wide assortment of equipment at prices ranging from less than £10 to more than £300. Each unit has its advantages and its disadvantages; each has its devoted following in the treasure hunting fraternity; each has its manufacturer and retailers who will confidently claim the model ABC is superior to model XYZ. Most of them can back their claims with an impressive list of finds made by the users of that particular model, and I do not doubt that by the time this book is published new manufacturers and new retailers will have arrived on the scene with fresh claims and even more spectacular success stories about the new model they would like you to buy.

The reason for this apparent confusion is simply this: **Success at amateur treasure hunting with a metal detector depends on how you use the detector.** The price tag on the unit, the number of transistors in its circuitry, the depth at which it will locate a single coin— all of these considerations account for only 10 per cent of the detector's success rate. The remaining 90 per cent is accounted for by the individual who uses the machine. You cannot transform yourself into a successful treasure hunter by investing a couple of hundred pounds in a top-performance unit; nor can you dismiss the simplest and least expensive models as 'mere toys', because in the hands of enthusiasts such units can turn up a surprising number of worthwhile finds.

How can I advise you on the choice of a metal detector when so much depends on the way in which *you* use it?

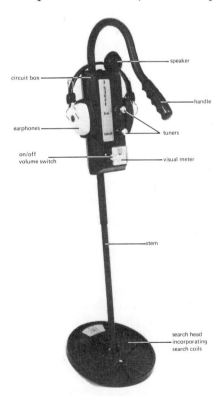

Fig. 18 The basic parts of a detector, shown on a C-Scope Mk. 3.

speaker

circuit box

handle

earphones

tuners

on/off
volume switch

visual meter

stem

search head
incorporating
search coils

The answer is, of course, that I cannot recommend a particular machine even though I am certain the model I use is best for *me*. To do so would be unfair to the manufacturers of other machines which might be ideally suited to your temperament, your pocket, and your interest in the hobby. If I recommended all readers should wear size seven wellington boots when working on a riverside those readers whose feet happen to fit that particular size would be happy; the majority would have ten sore toes. To recommend a particular detector as the ideal machine for every reader would be equally foolish. All I can do is relate my own experiences with metal detectors and offer you my opinions on the types best suited to particular applications. Some of you will be happy with the units I suggest; others will, I hope, find the units best suited to their needs by the time-honoured method of trial-and-error.

It is unnecessary to comprehend the electronic intricacies of the four basic circuits now used in the manufacture of amateur treasure hunting metal detectors, but a limited appreciation of the advantages and disadvantages of each system will help in deciding which system is best suited to your needs. The four basic circuits are:

Detector types

Beat frequency
Transmitter/receiver
Induction balance
Pulse induction.

Beat frequency (or BFO) detectors were the first amateur treasure hunting metal detectors to come on to the market, and all the machines at the lower end of the price scale are BFO units. This does not mean that BFO detectors are suitable only for children or those whose interest in the hobby is a passing fancy. Their low price does make them ideal detectors for those two groups; but many successful amateur treasure hunters find that inexpensive BFO units give them all they ask for in a detector, and many professionals use more sophisticated BFO units in preference to other machines. Numerous high-value finds (including The Grove Wood Treasure) have been made with BFO detectors costing less than £20.

The advantages of a well-designed, low cost, BFO unit used to locate coins and other small objects are:

1. It is simple to use.
2. It gives a quick and positive signal when locating a small object.
3. Its pin-pointing accuracy when indicating the spot where a coin is buried is a boon to all beginners.

Its disadvantages are:

1. Its depth penetration is not more than six inches for an object the size of a 10p piece.
2. The tuning knob on the unit requires regular adjustment throughout the search.

I stress that I am referring to the performance of a *well-designed* BFO unit. Poorly-designed BFO detectors have other disadvantages including a depth penetration of only one or two inches for a 10p piece, a signal note which 'warbles' constantly throughout the search whenever the head of the detector touches grass, and a tendency to give false signals when the head of the detector is warmed by strong sunlight. Manufacturers of well-designed BFO units overcome these problems by choosing the correct circuitry when designing the detector, and by the use of manufacturing materials which are not highly susceptible to expansion caused by temperature changes.

The need to make regular adjustments to the tuning control throughout the search is not a great disadvantage. Only a fractional movement of a small knob or tuning collar is required every few minutes; such minor adjustments being necessary on all Beat Frequency, Transmitter/Receiver and Induction Balance units because of the detector's tendency to *drift* slightly from the position you have selected on the tuner. This tuner can be compared to the steering wheel of a car which requires constant attention if the car is to be kept on a straight course. Metal detectors give maximum depth penetration only when tuners are carefully and delicately controlled.

Most beginners take the depth at which a detector can locate a single coin as the all-important consideration when deciding which model to buy. This has resulted in many newcomers to the hobby buying complicated and expensive units which they are incapable of handling correctly and which, because of their owners' inexperience, fail to locate those deeper objects which they imagine they must find to be successful at amateur treasure hunting. In my opinion most beginners do better if they disregard depth penetration when buying their first unit and look instead for a model which is simple to operate and which will pinpoint finds (however shallow) with a clear and unmistakable signal. That is, in fact, exactly what a well-designed and inexpensive BFO unit will do.

I have said that some professional treasure hunters are enthusiastic users of BFO units. The sophisticated instruments they use cost three or four times the price of simple BFO detectors; the higher cost resulting from improvements to the circuitry which give a depth penetration of approximately nine inches on a 10p piece, and which also reduce (but do not eliminate) the problems of drift. Most of the professionals who use advanced BFO units are dedicated coinshooters who have found the extremely fast reaction of BFO circuitry to single coins ideally suited to their need to find large numbers of single coins in a very short time on a wide variety of sites.

Transmitter/Receiver (or T/R) detectors. All metal detectors transmit and receive an electronic signal and might, therefore, be described as T/R units; but most manufacturers who sell their detectors under the T/R label are indicating that circuitry and search head coils are more sophisticated in design than are the circuits and search heads of BFO units. The result is an improvement in depth penetration and a reduction in drift.

T/R detectors are very similar in circuitry to Induction Balance units. The T/R circuit is slightly less expensive to produce and the signal it emits when finding a coin, which sounds very much like a BFO signal, makes it an easy unit to operate. On the other hand, T/R detectors designed for general coinshooting do not have the depth penetration of well-designed Induction Balance units in spite of the fact that they cost almost as much to buy. T/R detectors are at their best when they are designed to locate large objects at great depths (e.g. a pot of coins at four feet).

The advantages of a T/R unit are:

1. It has good depth penetration on large objects.
2. It gives a clear signal when locating a find.
3. It has less drift than a BFO unit.
4. It is fairly easy to operate.

Its disadvantages are:

1. When used for general coinshooting it does not equal a well-designed Induction Balance unit in performance even though it costs almost as much to buy.

Some American manufacturers describe their Transmitter/Receiver detectors as having 'T/R circuitry with balanced mutual induction bridge'. This description is correct, but it can mislead beginners who sometimes imagine they are purchasing true Induction Balance units when they read the sales literature. Bear in mind that the abbreviation, T/R, indicates that although the circuitry in the detector is similar to Induction Balance circuitry, it is less costly to manufacture and, in my opinion, less versatile when applied to amateur treasure hunting.

Occasionally you will see the letters T.R. used to describe BFO detectors having complex search heads which incorporate several search coils of different sizes. In this case the letters stand for 'Total Response' and they indicate that the detector is designed to find single coins *and* large objects at great depths while using the same search head. My opinion is that such detectors do not compare in performance with detectors having single or interchangeable coils.

Fig. 19 Note multi-coil search head on this Induction Balance unit, the Granger 'Questor'.

Induction balance (or IB) detectors are relative new-comers to the British amateur treasure hunting scene, though they have been firm favourites in the United States for a number of years. If well designed they are much more stable in operation than are BFO units, and depth penetration is approximately ten inches for a 10p piece. They do, however, require very patient and careful use if maximum benefit is to be derived from their sophisticated circuitry and multi-coil loops. In the hands of absolute beginners IB units can fail miserably at finding valuable objects; whereas almost anyone can find coins with a BFO unit after half an hour's practice with the machine. For this reason I hesitate to recommend IB detectors to beginners unless they are absolutely sure that their interest in amateur treasure hunting can sustain a period of two or three months during which the number of finds made with the detector will probably be very small. After this initial period—during which you must, of course, learn to handle the unit correctly—the number of finds you make will increase dramatically and you will begin to understand why IB detectors are used by so many professional treasure hunters.

It is worth noting that in spite of the fact that British treasure hunters were slow to appreciate IB circuitry there are now a number of excellent British-made IB detectors on the market.

The advantages of an IB unit are:

1. It has greater depth penetration than a BFO or T/R detector.
2. It has greater tuning stability than a BFO detector.

Its disadvantages are:

1. It requires very careful use if maximum benefit is to be derived from its superior coinshooting capabilities.

Pulse induction is the latest innovation in circuitry design to reach the treasure hunting world and its arrival has caused much controversy in professional circles. Pulse detectors have exceptional depth penetration; they can locate a 10p piece at depths in excess of twelve inches with incredible ease. They are also totally free from drift problems and there can be no doubt that their integrated and highly complex circuitry makes Pulse machines far superior metal detectors to any of the types mentioned above.

Alas, they have, in my opinion, two major disadvantages when used for amateur treasure hunting which you should consider most carefully before you buy. Firstly, they are exceptionally sensitive to iron; a Pulse machine will easily find a small nail or fragment of scrap iron at a depth of ten inches. Most beginners and many electronics experts who know little or nothing about amateur treasure hunting do not regard this exceptional iron sensitivity as a great disadvantage because they fail to appreciate how many small fragments of iron there are on the majority of sites used by amateur treasure hunters. They consider only the possibility of finding coins and other valuable metal objects at great depths. In practice so much time is spent recovering the scrap iron which Pulse machines find that the improvement in depth penetration on coins, rings, and other worthwhile finds cannot be used to full advantage.

Against this it must be said that Pulse machines are unaffected by silver paper which BFO, T/R, and IB detectors *do* find. However, 80 per cent of all silver paper on sites other than beaches is to be found on the surface or just below grass roots. A BFO, T/R, or IB user quickly spots that he has detected silver paper and rarely has to dig it up.

The second major disadvantage of Pulse units is, in my opinion, their poor pinpointing capabilities. BFO, T/R, and IB units will, when well designed, indicate *exactly* where an object is buried; Pulse units will merely indicate the presence of a metal object in the general area of the search head.

There is one type of amateur treasure hunting site on which Pulse units can be used to great advantage by amateur treasure hunters. This is on beaches which are relatively free from iron fragments but which are usually contaminated by large amounts of silver paper. On such sites the Pulse detector's insensitivity to silver paper and its exceptional depth penetration make it an ideal tool.

The advantages of a Pulse unit are:

1. It has exceptional depth penetration.
2. It is free from drift.
3. It is insensitive to silver paper.

Its disadvantages are:

1. It is highly sensitive to iron.
2. It has poor pinpointing capabilities.

Developments in detector circuitry are continuous. Many experts are now at work improving and modifying

49

existing circuitry in order to improve your chances of valuable finds when using your detector as an amateur treasure hunting tool. My comments on BFO, T/R, IB and Pulse detectors are, I believe, accurate at the time of writing. Keep up to date on developments by reading magazines such as *True Treasure Monthly* which report regularly on innovations in detector design and circuitry.

Extras   In addition to a choice of detectors working on the principles outlined above, all of which are available in a very wide price range, the beginner can also buy a model equipped with such refinements as visual meters, headphones, extra search coils, special tuners, and waterproofed heads. On some models these are standard equipment; on others they are available as optional extras.

I have not found a visual meter to be a great asset when coinshooting, though some treasure hunters do find them useful. In my opinion a detector user's eyes should remain on the search head when a piece of ground is being surveyed. This is difficult when one's eyes must also watch a flickering needle on a meter fitted close to the handle of the machine.

Headphones are extremely useful, though I do know many successful treasure hunters who never use them. The types which fit snuggly over the head are more comfortable in use than are the 'stethoscopic' types which fit around the neck. Some of the less expensive models are equipped with an ear-piece which the user pushes into his ear.

Additional search coils which can be interchanged with the standard coil are available on a number of models. Usually a search coil of approximately six inches diameter will already be fitted to the model you buy. This is an ideal coin hunting size, but it is unsuitable for hunting larger objects at depths beyond two feet. A search coil of ten or twelve inches diameter must be fitted when searching for larger objects. As this will *not* find single coins it becomes necessary to have two (or more) coils if large and small objects are to be found at various depths. Changing the search coils is a simple operation which usually requires nothing more than the removal and re-tightening of one or two screws or nuts.

Many IB and T/R units have multi-coil search heads which can be used to hunt both large and small objects without the need for interchangeable heads.

Refinements to the tuner on a detector are almost always an asset; any detector which has extra-fine tuning features is worth considering. On many units these are now standard equipment.

Waterproof detectors are an obvious asset in countries such as Britain where even the most careful precautions cannot rule out the possibility of being caught in an unexpected storm with your detector exposed to the dangers of rainwater penetration. A large plastic bag should always be carried as insurance against such emergencies whether or not your detector is waterproofed.

'Water immersible' does not mean the same as water-proofed. A water-immersible unit can be used to search

Fig. 20 Water immersible detectors are extremely useful on riversides and beaches.

rivers and shallow sea water by placing the head and stem of the detector in water to a point just below the circuit box beneath the handle. This is an extremely useful feature when treasure hunting along riversides and on beaches and I recommend water-immersible detectors to all readers who plan to search such sites.

Finally, there are the 'luxury' items such as carrying cases and wheeled trolleys which are available with more expensive models. Whether or not you buy them depends on the amount you wish to spend. In my opinion it is better to use the few extra pounds that such luxuries would add to the bill in order to buy a more sophisticated basic unit.

Buying your first detector From time to time organizations such as the British Amateur Treasure Hunting Club hold widely publicized meetings which usually take the form of large-scale treasure hunts on riversides and public beaches. If you attend one of these meetings you will have an opportunity to see a large number of different metal detectors in action; you will be able to talk to their owners about performance, finds made, and the general usability of each model. At some meetings it is possible to hire a detector for an hour on payment of a small hire charge. This is an excellent method of trying out a machine before you decide to buy.

Most detector suppliers also offer a hire service on the models they stock. A detector can be hired for as little as £1 per day, and it can also be mailed to your home if you live some distance from the nearest supplier. Such hire services are particularly useful if you wish to take a metal detector on holiday in order to try it out on sites you might visit during your stay at the resort; by using a hired model for several hours each day during your stay you will be able to reach some conclusions about its suitability to your requirements.

An increasing number of suppliers now offer a 'seven-days-trial' service on all machines in their range. This service allows you to obtain a detector and to use it for one week before making a final decision to confirm your purchase. You must, of course, ensure that the unit is returned to the supplier promptly and in good condition should you decide not to buy.

All three services—the short hire during an organized treasure hunt, the long-term hire for holiday use, and the seven-days-trial—are useful in helping newcomers decide on the model they will buy. They should not, however, be used to form fixed opinions on the ultimate capabilities of a particular model. As I have already said, it can take many months to master the techniques of operating sophisticated metal detectors as amateur treasure hunting tools. You should only use the above services for a quick check on the detector's weight, its stem length in relation to your arm length, accessibility of control switches, and other physical considerations. Reliable conclusions on its amateur treasure hunting capabilities can only be reached after several months of diligent and prolonged use on a wide variety of sites.

There is one other method of obtaining information on the range of detectors currently available. Send stamped and self-addressed envelopes to every supplier and you will receive, by return post, price lists, catalogues, and other useful literature which will enable you to make your own list of all available models which are sold within your particular price range. I recommend this as a step which all newcomers should take.

Your first search

I am prepared to bet my best pair of boots that every reader who buys a detector will rush into his garden or on to the nearest piece of waste ground the moment he gets the unit home in order to confirm that it does indeed find pieces of metal buried beneath the soil. Some will even hide coins under carpets and locate them with their 'electronic bloodhounds' to the delight and amazement of the entire family. If it does nothing else, this first test will familiarize you with the controls on the unit—though I did hear of one man who found a gold coin within five minutes of becoming a detector owner.

Once you have satisfied your initial curiosity I would like you to return to this book to read and memorize the amateur treasure hunters' Code of Conduct which follows. It is probably the most important piece of information this book contains, and until you have memorized it *and* accepted it as a code by which you will abide you cannot call yourself an amateur treasure hunter. If you fail to observe the rules which it lays down you will fail to make valuable finds and you might also do harm to the hobby.

The amateur treasure hunters' Code of Conduct

1. Don't interfere with archaeological sites or ancient monuments. Join your local archaeological society if you are interested in ancient history.
2. Don't leave a mess. It is perfectly simple to extract a coin or other small object buried a few inches under the ground without digging a great hole. Use a sharpened trowel or knife to cut a neat circle; extract the object; replace the soil and grass carefully and even *you* will have difficulty in finding the spot again.
3. Help keep Britain tidy—and help yourself. Bottle tops, silver paper and tin cans are the last things you should throw away. You could well be digging them up again next year. So do yourself and the community a favour by taking all rusty junk you find to the nearest litter bin.
4. Don't trespass. Ask permission before venturing on to any private land.
5. Report all unusual historical finds to your local museum and get expert help if you accidentally discover a site of archaeological interest.
6. Learn the Treasure Trove laws and report all finds of gold and silver objects to the police. You will be well rewarded if the objects you find are declared Treasure Trove.
7. Respect the Country Code. Don't leave gates open when crossing fields and don't damage crops or frighten animals.

8. Never miss an opportunity to show and explain your detector to anyone who asks about it. Be friendly. You could pick up some clues to a good site.
9. If you meet another detector user while out on a hunt introduce yourself. You could probably teach each other a lot.
10. Finally, remember that when you are out with your detector you are an ambassador for the whole amateur treasure hunting fraternity. Don't give us a bad name.

The above code was written with the help of the Department of the Environment (Ancient Monuments Secretariat) at a time when the hobby of amateur treasure hunting was in its infancy and when *anyone* using a metal detector (other than the police, the army, and some industrial users) was referred to as 'a treasure hunter'. No distinction was made between amateur treasure hunters and amateur archaeologists; and because the latter used metal detectors to hunt for antiquities on recognized archaeological sites all detector users were branded by the Council for British Archaeology as 'looters' who caused irreparable damage to archaeological sites. It is of the utmost importance, therefore, that you appreciate the difference between an amateur archaeologist and an amateur treasure hunter.

Amateur archaeologists are interested in *antiquities*, and their activities are confined to archaeological sites. They should (though many do not) join their local archaeological society and surrender all finds made on archaeological 'digs' to the local society. They should use metal detectors under the supervision of a qualified archaeologist, and only on those areas of the 'dig' to which the qualified archaeologist directs them.

Amateur treasure hunters are interested in the recovery of lost, hidden, or discarded objects dating from the past three hundred years. Their activities are confined to beaches, riversides, footpaths, commons, houses, gardens and other *non-archaeological* sites. They collect coins, badges, buttons, bottles, and other *historically* interesting objects of eighteenth-, nineteenth-, and early twentieth-century origins. Co-incidentally they do find objects of archaeological significance—though *not* on archaeological sites. In this way archaeology has benefited from the activities of amateur treasure hunters who have, during the past few years, found a number of important pre-Roman, Roman, and Saxon coin hoards on public footpaths and in woods. These sites would never have been considered as interesting locations by archaeologists, because they were far away from known or suspected archaeological sites. The coins in those hoards have all found their way to public museums —though little appreciation of this assistance freely given to archaeology by amateur treasure hunters has been shown by the C.B.A.

To return to the first search, your initial trial of the detector's metal-finding capabilities should confirm that the unit is working correctly. By following the manufacturer's instructions you should be able to operate the controls efficiently and tune the instrument to its most sensitive setting. Equip yourself with a stout penknife, a long screwdriver, a large plastic bag to protect your instrument from rain, several small bags for your finds, and spare batteries for the detector. You are now ready for the hunt.

If you look at an early Ordnance Survey map of your area and compare it with a modern map covering the same piece of ground you will be able to locate many open spaces, footpaths and other interesting sites used by people living in and around your town in Victorian times. Consider a public footpath which winds its way across a common. In these days of motorways and motorcars the footpath might at first seem a most unlikely place to search for worthwhile finds; but modern appearances are often deceptive.

Most public footpaths date from at least the eighteenth century (some are much earlier) and if we estimate that only half a dozen people walked along your particular path every day between 1700 and 1900 we find that 438,000 pairs of feet tramped along it during those years. If only one person in one thousand lost or threw away a shoe buckle, a metal button, a ring, a coin, a badge, a hatpin, a brooch, or some other small metal object, there are 438 interesting finds to be made along the path. To find some of these 438 objects you must use the following amateur treasure hunting techniques.

You *must* resolve to carry out a thorough and painstaking search. It will take several days to search a footpath which is two or three miles in length so you should begin by making a sketch of the path on which you can mark features such as gates and trees to be used as reference points during the search. If you do not do this a thorough coverage of the site is made more difficult because it is very easy to forget which areas you searched on the previous day.

When you reach the point at which you decide to start the hunt pace out the distance across the width of the path *including* the area of grass one yard to left and right. If the path is one yard wide the width of your search area will, therefore, be three yards. Mark the starting point on the sketch, then switch on and tune in your detector.

As a newcomer to detector techniques you are likely to make three mistakes when searching your first site: You will not keep the head of the detector close enough to the ground; you will attempt to carry out your search too quickly; and you will be tempted to use a random search pattern instead of submitting to the discipline of a thorough search. *Any one of these mistakes will considerably reduce your chances of finding valuable objects.*

When you use a metal detector you *must* keep the head of the unit as close as possible to the ground. On grassy sites you should 'iron' the ground with the head; on gravel, pebbles, or other rough surfaces which might damage the detector you should ensure that the head of the unit is *never more than half an inch from the ground.* The detector must also be held in such a way that the search head remains parallel to the ground surface. Do not tilt the handle so that the front of the head is not level with its rear.

If you think it possible to search a couple of miles of public footpath in one afternoon you have not yet grasped

Fig. 21 (*top left*) Wrong. Head of detector too far off the ground.

Fig. 22 (*top right*) Wrong. Head of detector is not parallel to the ground.

Fig. 23 (*right*) Right. Head of detector is 'ironing' the ground. Note lines and pins used to search this open site.

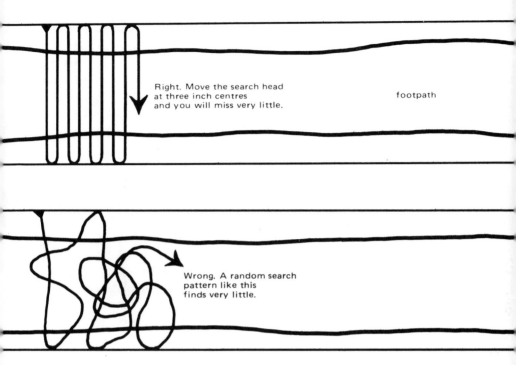

Right. Move the search head
at three inch centres
and you will miss very little.

footpath

Wrong. A random search
pattern like this
finds very little.

Fig. 24 Search pattern on
a footpath.

the basic principles of amateur treasure hunting; you are
still under the impression that you have purchased a 'magic
wand'. Your detector can only locate the valuables beneath
the surface of the footpath if *you* pass the search head over
those spots where valuables are buried. This cannot be
done during an afternoon stroll.

If you use a random search pattern you stand as much
chance of finding valuable objects with your detector as
you do of winning a dividend on a football pool. The
rewards from amateur treasure hunting go to those people
who possess the patience to search each site they visit with
absolute thoroughness. Make a determined effort to be
thorough on your first search and thoroughness will
become a habit. In this way you will soon build an impressive collection of worthwhile finds.

59

Start your search of the pathway at a point one yard from its edges. Keep the search head level with and as close as possible to the ground; walk *slowly* and *backwards* across the width of the path to a point one yard from the opposite edge. Now move the search head three inches to left or right of your first line and walk *slowly forwards* until you reach a point three inches to left or right of your original starting point. Continue this back and forth search across the path and its verges at three-inch intervals until your detector signals that a metal object is beneath the search head. Pinpoint the spot by moving the detector across the immediate area of the signal and then extract the object you have found.

On grass verges this should be done by first using your knife to cut a neat plug of turf approximately six inches in diameter around the point at which you obtained maximum signal strength. Put the plug to one side and check the exposed soil once again with the detector to confirm that the find has not been removed with the grass roots. If it is still in the ground probe the spot with your screwdriver until you feel the object; it can then be quickly and neatly extracted with a quick flick of the screwdriver blade.

Fig. 25 (*left*) It is quite unnecessary to make a mess when extracting a find. Cut a neat plug of turf with a sharp knife.

Fig. 26 (*right*) Use your detector to locate the find.

Fig. 27 Replace the grass plug when you have removed the metal object. Even *you* will have difficulty finding the spot again if you refill the hole in this way.

Check the spot once again with the detector because some objects, particularly coins, are often found close together; it is not uncommon to find half a dozen coins, one on top of the other, which have at some time in the past fallen from the same pocket or purse. When satisfied you have cleared the spot, replace the grass plug and press it down firmly with your foot. Remove every object you find on grassed sites by this method and any site you search will be left neat and tidy when you have completed your detector survey.

If the find is located on the bare footpath you should have little difficulty in flicking it out of the ground with the screwdriver blade. The bare earth can then be neatly pressed down again with your shoe. Develop the habit of carefully filling in each hole as soon as you have extracted the object and you will not need to re-trace your steps to fill in holes at the end of the day.

You should mark on your sketch the location of every find you make, and also make brief notes in the margin to indicate what each object is and, in the case of coins, their ages. In addition to providing a detailed record of your finds, this information will give you some idea of the sorts of finds you should make on other sites which have a similar history.

When you have made your first find, filled in the hole and recorded the details on your sketch, you are ready to continue the search. Do not wander off down the footpath admiring the coin, ring, or whatever it is you have found. Start again directly above the point at which you made the first find; work back and forth across the footpath at three-inch intervals; and at the end of your search you should have an impressive collection of objects which were lost, discarded, or possibly hidden along that site at some time during the past two or three centuries.

Searching open spaces   The techniques used to search open areas of grassland on commons and in the countryside are similar to those used to search footpaths; but the size of many of these sites makes an inch-by-inch search an impossible task for most amateur treasure hunters. Other methods have to be employed in order to locate those spots on the site which are most likely to yield the largest number of interesting finds.

Visit a common, a park, or any other stretch of open grassland on a sunny weekend and you will see hundreds of people relaxing and enjoying themselves. Observe the scene closely and it will soon become obvious that certain locations on the site are more popular than others. Large trees attract picnickers who use the tree as a convenient backrest; grassy slopes which command views of lakes, streams, and other focal points have more people sitting on them than have slopes which face less interesting views; children play their ball games on flat pieces of ground; while courting couples favour more secluded spots.

Imagine the same scene as it might have appeared in Victorian times. Little, apart from dress styles, would be changed. The picnickers would group around the largest trees; the Sunday strollers would rest on the grassy slopes to admire the view; the children would play on the same piece of ground; while the courting couples (more discreet, perhaps) would seek out the secluded spots. If the site is deep in the countryside, far away from any large town, and popular today only because it can be reached by car, the number of people using it now will be far greater than in Victorian times. However, the Victorians were great lovers of parks, open spaces, picnics, and all outdoor activities. A recreational site such as this which could be easily reached on foot from a town, or which was situated on a Victorian omnibus or train route, probably attracted even more visitors one hundred years ago than it does today.

It will be obvious to you that on such sites valuable finds are most likely to be made around large old trees, on grassy slopes facing interesting views, on play areas, and in secluded spots used by courting couples. These are the places where coins are most likely to have fallen from pockets and purses, where insecure fasteners on brooches and brace-lets are most likely to have failed their owners, and where thousands of people will have lost some object of value at some time in the past. Thus, half an hour's detective work spent on a quick survey of your chosen site *before* you use your metal detector can eliminate large areas of ground as relatively unproductive and pinpoint the locations on which your search should be concentrated.

Trees

The productive area around any old tree on the type of site we are now considering will extend from the base of the trunk to a point directly below the outer limits of the leaves. A circular search pattern should be used, starting at the base of the tree and working outwards at three-inch intervals until the entire area beneath the branches has been covered.

Grassy slopes

Coins and other valuables lost on grassy slopes usually find their way to the bottom of the slope—either shortly after being lost by simply rolling down the incline, or by move-ments in the soil over a longer period of time. If you concentrate your search around the lower slopes and search an area two or three yards wide using the same search

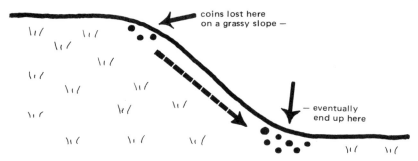

coins lost here
on a grassy slope —

— eventually
end up here

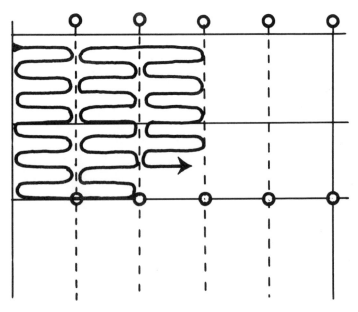

Fig. 28 (*top left*) Start your search around an old tree from the base of the trunk.

Fig. 29 (*top right*) Do not neglect grassy slopes. They hold a rich harvest of finds.

Fig. 30 (*centre*) The movement of coins on a slope.

Fig. 31 (*right*) Search pattern on a level site using lines and pins.

pattern as that used on footpaths you should soon make exciting finds.

It is difficult to carry out a thorough search on a level site **Level sites** more than a few yards wide without a set of lines and pins. These are similar to the lines and pins which bricklayers use to help them lay level courses of brickwork. You can make yourself a set with two pieces of string approximately twenty feet in length, the ends of which are tied to four pointed wooden stakes six inches long. Push the first pair of stakes into the ground twenty feet apart and position the second pair one yard to left or right so that the two pieces of string form a parallel-sided pathway across the site. You can now search the area between the string lines with your detector by using the footpath search method. When you have searched this area thoroughly the first two stakes are moved one yard left or right of the second set to mark out the next area. Thus, the entire site can be thoroughly covered.

It is impossible to lay down firm rules for searching such **Secluded spots** spots because the secluded locations on every site you visit will be different. Your own observations coupled with the search methods outlined above should suggest the best technique to employ. All that can be said with certainty is that secluded spots more than repay the attention given them by amateur treasure hunters. They are always rich in valuable finds.

Many commons and areas of woodland open to the **Jewellery** public are criss-crossed by narrow footpaths which link areas of particular beauty or interest. On a large number of sites these paths cut their way up and down some very steep slopes. If your site has such features you should mark the steepest pathways as important search areas because they are most likely to be rich in lost jewellery.

On sites other than public beaches most rings, bracelets, and brooches are lost when the wearer trips, stumbles, or falls. This is most likely to happen when climbing or descending steep and often slippery pathways. If you carry

65

out a thorough search on both sides of a steep pathway you should find modern rings, brooches, and bracelets; if you carry out an equally thorough search of the area around the bottom of the slope you should also find Victorian and possibly earlier jewellery.

I must stress once again the importance of removing the objects you find in the ground in such a way that any site you search is left neat and tidy at the end of the day. Rule 2 of the Code of Conduct must be strictly observed at all times.

Finding new sites Your success with a metal detector depends almost entirely on the amount of research you undertake to locate possible sites and on how carefully you cover those areas which your research indicates as good hunting grounds. Your local library has, or can obtain for you, all the research material you will need to find excellent sites in your area. Bear in mind that you are looking for commons, footpaths, and open spaces which have been accessible to the public for two or three hundred years. Old maps and local history books will tell you where to find them and who used them or visited them in the past. What you find there then depends on how thoroughly you search for the objects which have been lost, discarded, or hidden there during the past three centuries.

4 Treasure hunting on the coast

Those 'miles of golden sand' described in publicity leaflets put out by seaside holiday resorts often turn out to be rather less attractive than the glossy photograph on the leaflet would have us believe. Nevertheless, I endorse the publicity officers' claims; the sand is 'golden', but the gold lies a few inches beneath the surface. It is the durable, valuable, and highly-prized variety which men have sought in mountains and deserts throughout the world for the past few thousand years, and substantial amounts of it lie under that not-so-golden sand around our coasts.

Approximately 500,000 items of personal jewellery are lost on Britain's beaches every year. Some fall from handbags, purses, and pockets when their owners undress, sit in deckchairs, or play games on the seafront; others are lost from wrists, necks, and fingers during plunges into the sea, and most readers will have added their contribution to this lost treasure on our shores. Similar losses have occurred since Benjamin Beale of Margate invented the bathing machine in 1780. How, then, can you go about finding your share of this seaside bonanza?

Sand sifting

As we have already concluded from our observations of human behaviour on commons and in parks, most people are gregarious by nature. On wide stretches of open grassland they congregate thickly on a few spots which are preferred, however crowded they may become, because they offer better views, convenient backrests, or ideal play areas. On beaches the sites which holidaymakers choose to pitch their tents, windbreaks, and deckchairs are selected with similar human considerations in mind. Most of the deckchairs will be set up within a few hundred yards of the attendant's hut; the sand in the vicinity of the tea stalls and roundabouts will be thick with prostrate bodies and rowdy children; while any sea wall which provides a ready-made backrest will be a highly favoured location. If there are sand dunes nearby there you will find most of the courting couples. Meanwhile, vast expanses of 'golden sand' will

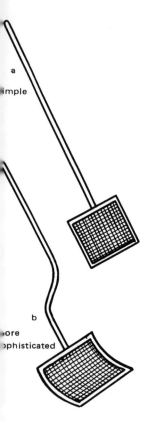

Fig. 32 Sand sifter.

remain quite deserted throughout the holiday season.

Obviously these popular locations will hold the majority of recent losses. Any coin, ring, brooch, or other valuable object accidently dropped in the soft sand hereabouts will be buried in seconds, usually before the owner realizes the loss. If you search these sites in the evening after the crowds have dispersed you will soon discover just how careless people are with their money and with their personal possessions. Recent losses will lie only a few inches beneath the surface of the sand and you can locate them very easily with a metal detector. Alternatively you can make a simple sand sifter which is an ideal tool for searching soft, dry sand.

It consists of a lightweight wooden frame approximately one yard wide and one foot in length which is covered by quarter-inch wire netting. The frame is attached to a strong broom handle which must be long enough to enable the wire covered frame to rest on the sand at an angle of less than forty-five degrees. A more sophisticated sifter might have a curved frame and a handle shaped as in Fig. 13b.

In use the sifter is pushed across the selected search area so that the leading edge of the frame digs into the soft sand. Do not hold the handle at too steep an angle otherwise it will become difficult to push. Aim at skimming the top three inches of sand and carry out a methodical search of each area by raking at one-yard intervals and by using a search pattern similar to that used with a metal detector on a footpath.

Finding older coins and jewellery

A search of the top three inches of soft sand carried out on the most popular locations on your beach will reveal large amounts of modern coinage and jewellery lost by recent visitors. If you wish to make earlier finds you must first learn something of the way in which objects lost on beaches are moved by the natural forces at work on the coastline.

Consider the high, dry sand at the top of the beach. If this is never (or only very rarely) covered by an incoming tide objects lost there will simply sink deeper beneath the surface over a long period of time. You cannot find these deeper objects with a sand sifter because the sand twelve

Fig. 33 A Pulse induction detector has the range to locate deep objects buried beneath the high, dry sand at the top of the beach. This is a Geo-Electronics C440.

inches down is too damp and clinging to pass through the wire mesh. A Pulse induction detector *would* be extremely useful on such a site; with it you would probably locate large numbers of single coins and items of jewellery to a depth of twelve or even fifteen inches. At that depth Victorian coins are almost certain to be found; but many heavier gold coins and larger pieces of jewellery will sink beyond twelve inches on this type of site.

If you dig a fairly deep hole on a beach you will see that the sand uncovered two or three feet beneath the surface is compressed by the weight of sand above it. This compressed material looks and feels like soft sandstone and you will be able to dig it out in lumps. Treasure hunters call it 'hard-pack' and they are always very interested to learn at what depth it occurs on each coastal site they visit because they know that any valuables originally lost on those parts of the beach not covered by the tide will eventually come to rest on top of the hard-pack.

Some years ago a treasure hunting acquaintance of mine was at work on a beach in southern England at a time when a gang of workmen were repairing the sea wall nearby. A mechanical shovel was being used to clear sand from the top of the beach so that new stonework could be built. When the shovel dug into the beach it removed several cubic yards of sand to expose a wide area of hard-pack. This was covered by hundreds of rings, watches, gold spectacle frames, Victorian brooches, sovereigns, and silver coins. Needless to say, my acquaintance had a very profitable day!

Fig. 34 Section through a beach.

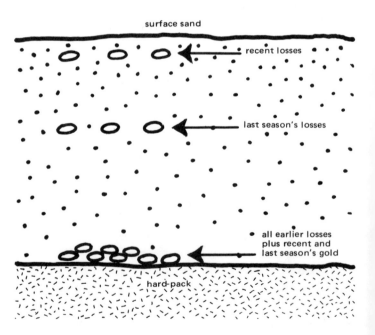

Plate 1 Clay tobacco pipes and printed pot lids from an old dump in Buckinghamshire. Pipes with ornate bowls were fashionable between 1880 and 1900; printed pot lids were used throughout Victoria's reign.

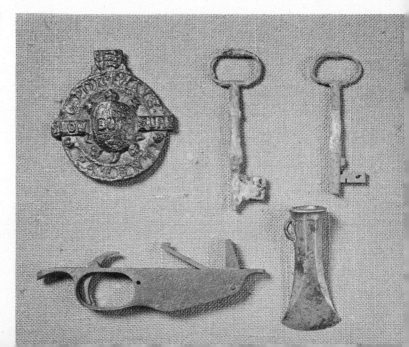

Plate 2 The axehead, found on the site of an ancient ford, dates from BC 50; the trigger mechanism is from a weapon made 1900 years later. The keys and ornate fire back were recovered from an old house which was due for demolition.

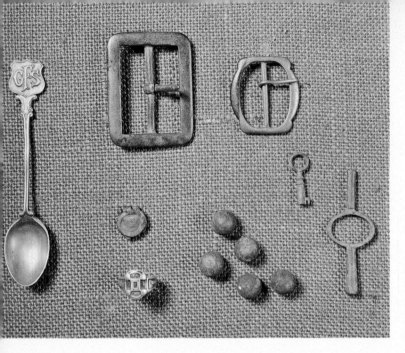

Plate 3 Rings, cutlery, keys, buckles and musket balls—typical of the finds you can expect to make on any site which has been used by large numbers of people for several hundred years. Those shown here come from a London common.

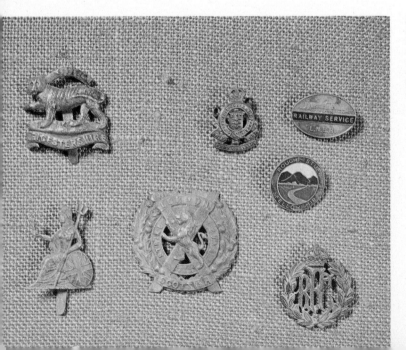

Plate 4 Impressive collections of military badges can be made by searching parks, riversides and public beaches with a metal detector. Somewhat less common are finds of ordinary lapel badges.

There are, of course, many valuable finds to be made between the surface and the hard-pack; it can be generally said that the deeper you dig on a beach the older will be the coins you find. But unless you get down to the hard-pack you stand little chance of finding gold coins or gold jewellery because this metal, being exceptionally heavy, sinks to the hard-pack soon after being lost.

The best search method on such a site is to use a wide shovel, a shallow wooden or plastic tray, and a metal detector. It is strenuous work and for this reason I recommend that you concentrate your hunt on those areas which produced the greatest number of finds when you used your sand sifter. We know that human nature can be regarded as a fairly constant factor so it is reasonable to assume that people who visited the site fifty or one hundred years ago lost most of their valuables on the same stretch of beach.

Dig out a trench one yard wide and three yards long and go down until you hit the hard-pack. As you dig fill up the tray with sand you remove and pass the head of the detector over it. If you do not obtain a signal from the detector you can throw the sand out of the tray and re-fill it again. In this way each shovelful can be thoroughly checked and you are unlikely to miss any valuables you dig out. When you have removed one cubic yard of sand back-fill the hole by throwing sand behind you each time you empty the tray. At the end of the search you should be left with only a small hole which you can fill in with the sand you dug out to start the trench.

Tides

I said at the beginning of this chapter that many items of jewellery lost on public beaches every year slip from wrists, necks, and fingers during plunges into the sea. It is a fact that fingers on hands which are suddenly immersed in cold seawater after being warmed by summer sunshine contract so that rings become loose and are very likely to slip off. Throwing oneself in wild abandon into the foaming brine also puts a severe strain on safety catches holding necklaces and bracelets and many fail their owners shortly after entering the water. Valuable objects lost in this manner are

71

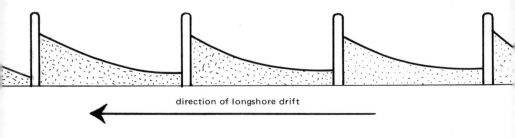

direction of longshore drift

Fig. 35 Build-up of sand against groynes.

moved by tides and currents in the same way as are objects lost on riversides. Fortunately it is possible to predict with some accuracy where they will eventually come to rest.

Readers of my earlier book, *Pebble Polishing*, will know the phenomenon known as Longshore Drift carries pebbles along a beach in a particular direction which is determined by the geographical location of the beach. In Britain it can be generally stated that the direction of Longshore Drift on East coast beaches is from north to south; on West coast beaches it is from south to north; and on South coast beaches it is from west to east. You can confirm the direction of drift on your beach by examining the piles of sand which always build up against any groynes which have been constructed to resist the movement of sand by Longshore Drift. The sand will always be deeper on one side of the groynes and this is the direction from which loose material is being carried by the tides.

Once you know the direction of drift on your particular beach carry out a detector search along the high tide line near the most popular bathing spot. Follow the line in the direction of Longshore Drift and you will soon begin to find lost valuables amongst the driftwood and other debris which marks the highest point reached by the previous tide.

Currents   We have seen that the direction of flow in a river is determined by the shape of the riverbed. Bumps, depressions, and other obstructions set up eddy currents which cause coins and other valuables to be deposited at certain

72

points along the riverbank. These rules apply equally to beaches, and it is a thorough understanding of their implications which enables beachcombers to be so remarkably successful at finding lost valuables.

I heard recently a story concerning a beachcomber living in Cornwall which illustrates the skill these old men have developed by a thorough study of the natural forces at work on their local beaches. A friend of mine had the misfortune to lose a valuable signet ring while bathing on a holiday beach in Cornwall. He had taken his metal detector with him on his trip and he spent two days hunting the ring without success. On the afternoon of the second day a weather-beaten old man approached him and asked what he was doing with his 'electronic gadget'. Somewhat impatiently my friend explained his problem and was taken aback when the Cornishman replied, 'Don't think much of your gadget, but tell me exactly where you lost the ring and I'll find it for you. It'll cost you a pound.'

My friend was due to leave the following day and he knew his chances of finding the ring in the few hours of daylight which remained were slim. Silently he handed over a pound note and then walked with the old man to the spot where he had been swimming when the ring slipped from his finger. The old man looked at the area for a few moments before holding up the pound note and tearing it in half. He handed one half back to my astonished friend and said, 'She'll come up in her own good time down by the harbour wall. Give me your name and address and I'll post it on to you. Send the other half of the note when you get it.'

Five months went by before my friend heard from the old beachcomber again. He had almost forgotten the incident when, on a wintery morning in November, the postman delivered a small box to his home. Inside was his signet ring and a note from the old man which read, 'Sorry it took so long. Weather's been too mild lately. Had to wait for the first winter gale. Send other half of note. Good luck with your gadget.'

Stand on the sea wall or on some other vantage point near your particular beach at low tide and look carefully at the

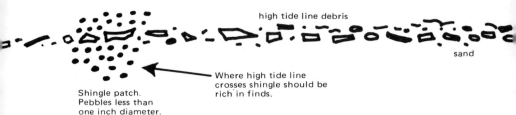

high tide line debris

sand

Where high tide line
crosses shingle should be
rich in finds.

Shingle patch.
Pebbles less than
one inch diameter.

low water mark

sea

Fig. 36 A beach 'glory
hole'.

area of sand between high and low water marks. You may
see shallow pools of water left by the falling tide. They
indicate depressions in the beach which cause eddy currents
and you will find a thorough search in and around these
pools with your detector highly productive of good finds.

You should also look out for isolated patches of shingle on
the beach. If the pebbles in it are approximately one inch in
diameter the sand beneath them is very likely to hold coins
and other lost objects deposited there by a current which for
some reason became too weak to carry coins, jewellery, and
small pebbles at that particular spot. Deep digging on these
locations can be very profitable, especially when the
shingle patch is crossed by a high tide line. Modern coins
and jewellery will also have been deposited here and the site
will have become a 'glory hole' rich in valuable finds. These
are the secrets which successful beachcombers have taught
themselves by careful observation. Use them with patience
and you can confidently expect similar success.

**Wintertime
treasure hunting**   An open beach in winter can be bitterly cold, especially
when a gale is blowing onto the shore. Nevertheless, I urge
you to visit your beach site as often as possible from Novem-

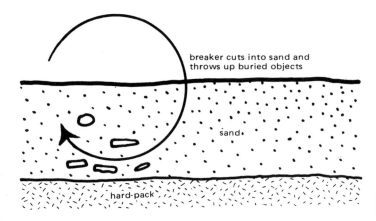

breaker cuts into sand and
throws up buried objects

sand.

hard-pack

Fig. 37 The power of a
breaking wave.

ber to February if you are determined to succeed at treasure
hunting on the coast. Stand on a beach when a storm is
blowing and you will see the breakers literally ploughing
the sand as they smash onto the shoreline. Valuables lost
on the site during the previous holiday season are churned
up by the waves; on some sites it is actually possible to see
coins and rings dancing up the beach as the breakers throw
them forward—a sight worth seeing in spite of the savage
wind and stinging foam!

In order to work a beach in wintertime it is essential that
you are equipped with a water-immersible detector, warm
and waterproof clothing, and a pair of waders. You should
also bear in mind that many cafés and snackbars are likely
to be closed in the middle of winter. Add hot drinks and
sandwiches to your list of essentials when visiting smaller
resorts.

Weather forecasts and local coastguard stations will
provide you with information on the possibility of rough
seas around the resort you intend to visit. When you hear
that a storm is imminent you must get down to the beach as
quickly as possible with your metal detector. Work at the
water's edge and follow the tide up and down the beach,
concentrating most of your attention on the few yards of
wet sand immediately above the breaking waves. Particu-

75

larly violent storms will sometimes send breakers crashing over the high, dry sand at the top of the beach which is not normally covered by the tide. When this happens the sea will do the strenuous digging work normally required to reach the hard-pack and you will find a rich harvest of valuables very near the surface if you search the site immediately after the storm subsides. High tide lines are equally productive after violent storms.

Wreck sites

In the romantic days of sail when men-of-war, frigates, sloops, East Indiamen, brigs, packets, schooners, and ketches braved the open seas at the mercy of the wind countless numbers of ships were wrecked around our coasts. Navigation at the time was most inadequate; the first ship's chronometer did not appear until 1772 and navigation charts were either unreliable or dangerously misleading. (When Sir Cloudsley Shovel's famous and ill-fated ship, the *Association*, struck the western rocks of the Scillies in 1707 she was forty miles off course). Because of this a visual sighting of land was the only certain method of determining a ship's position. This required ships to sail close to shore in bad weather conditions—a practice which inevitably resulted in thousands of vessels running aground or smashing themselves to pieces on rocky coasts.

The greatest fear of all who sailed the open seas in those days was to be caught inshore with an on-shore wind

Fig. 38 A ship driven onto lee shore.

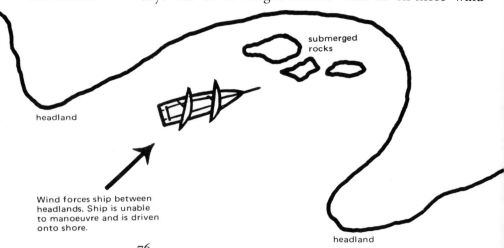

submerged rocks

headland

Wind forces ship between headlands. Ship is unable to manoeuvre and is driven onto shore.

headland

76

blowing the vessel to inevitable destruction because it could not sail clear of land. Sometimes, in a wild attempt to avert such a disaster, the captain of a ship would drop anchor and haul down his sails to reduce resistance to the wind. If the anchor cables parted, as they often did in the days when ropes were used, the ship was then helpless against the power of the storm. The master would try to reach an open beach before the vessel struck, but more often than not he would hit submerged rocks before reaching the shallows or swing broadside to the shore and capsize. Such a fate has overtaken thousands of ships on British shores.

Newcomers to amateur treasure hunting often imagine such phrases as 'thousands of wrecks' to be wishful thinking on the part of over-enthusiastic treasure hunters. If you think that let me quote to you from an article on British shipwrecks which appeared in *True Treasure Monthly* in November 1972. The article included a newspaper account of shipwrecks for the year 1860. It read:

> Last year (1860) was unprecedented for the succession of bad weather and the number of wrecks on the coast of Britain, and we have to report that the total number of wrecks is 146 up on the annual average for the previous six years. There were 541 wrecks totally lost, and 838 partially lost, making a total of 1,379 vessels employing 9,816 hands, and having a total tonnage of 215,000. The total estimated cargo value amounted to £603,065 and the total number of lives lost is 536. This last figure, we are pleased to report, is 264 under the average for the previous nine years.

If we take the average wreck figure mentioned for the years 1854–59 (1,233) we can calculate that during those *six* years no less than 7,398 vessels were wrecked around the coastline of Britain. Many of the ships were small coastal traders carrying cargoes of timber, iron ore, corn, and similar goods, while some carried cargoes which included gold and silver; but, rich or commonplace, they all added to the store of valuables which lie within a few yards of the shore.

The sites of some of the most spectacular treasure wrecks which litter our coasts are well known and they have attracted many divers and treasure hunters during the past few years. There are, however, very many valuable wrecks which have never been found. The only clues to their locations have come when a beachcomber or treasure hunter has found gold coins, silver ingots, or other valuable objects which could be approximately dated to the time of the particular wreck thought to lie in the shallow water just off shore. The most recent report I have of beach finds probably associated with an unrecorded wreck comes from Suffolk where gold coins of Edward III have recently turned up in the sand around Easton Barents. If, during your hunts for Victorian and modern coinage on public beaches, you find earlier coins which are unlikely to have been lost by holidaymakers you should mark the site as worthy of a thorough search during winter. It is when violent weather strikes the shore that the sea is most likely to throw up some of her hidden fortune at the feet of a determined treasure hunter.

5 Hunting for hoards

My records show that five valuable hoards were found by metal detector users during the first two months of 1973. They included a small bag of sovereigns, £10,000 in banknotes wrapped in tinfoil, an earthenware jar containing 1,000 gold and silver medieval coins, a hoard of nineteenth-century silverware, and a bronze pot containing over 5,000 Roman coins. No doubt there were others which I did not hear about, and there will certainly be many more equally exciting finds made before the end of the year.

In Britain (and in all other European countries) people have been hiding money and valuables in the ground or in their homes for more than 3,000 years. Banking is a recent innovation. Until the early part of the twentieth century most people kept their fortunes close to hand; the idea of giving money, plate, jewellery, or anything else of value to someone who would be paid to keep it safe was quite unthinkable. One looked after one's own and trusted no one.

It is difficult for us, living as we do in the relative security of the mid-twentieth century, to appreciate this urge to hoard which obsessed our ancestors. The Welfare State and three square meals a day tend to make us forget that life was precarious, dangerous, and unpredictable for most people who lived more than three or four generations ago. Tribal wars, invasions, military occupations, border strife, anarchy, sackings, looting, religious and political persecutions, plagues, famines, civil war, death by fire and sword—all have contributed to the vast amounts of gold, silver, coins, jewellery, and plate which have been hidden over the centuries. Add to this the basic human desire to have a sum of money, however small, put by for the inevitable rainy day and you will begin to understand why so much hoarding went on in the past.

Even today the necessity to hide wealth is still with us. Underworld rogues and thieves still bury their loot; tax evaders must find safe places to hide their undeclared income; and countless thousands of old ladies still prefer a teapot or the underside of a mattress to a smiling bank manager. I am confident that some readers of this book are thinking at this very moment of a little nest-egg tucked away in a secret hole in or around the home. Only they know why and where it is hidden and I do not propose to cause embarrassment by suggesting reasons or likely locations. Nevertheless, I can't help wondering . . .

Several hundred hoards were accidentally discovered in Britain between 1900 and 1970. If metal detectors and amateur treasure hunting had not grown to their present popularity it is likely that these accidental discoveries would have continued to occur at the steady rate of approximately half a dozen each year. Most of them were found by farmers, building workers, or demolition contractors who, by the nature of their occupations, spend much of their lives digging the earth or pulling down old buildings. There were, however, some notable exceptions. Children, being inquisitive and observant, have found their share of buried wealth, and the post-war booms in do-it-yourself and gardening have encouraged many householders to carry out structural repairs in their homes and deep digging in their gardens. This has turned up some exciting hoards which would otherwise have been found by builders and farmers. Let us recall a few of these accidental finds to see if they can teach us anything about where we should look in the hope of finding a hoard ourselves. These brief accounts are, incidentally, taken at random from the files of *True Treasure Monthly* where several hundred similar stories are on record.

In 1946 a lady in Hull decided to sweep the chimney in one of her bedrooms. When she pushed the brush up the flue she dislodged a biscuit tin containing £600 in notes.

In the same year a man living in Newcastle-under-Lyme was carrying out repairs to a bedroom floor when he discovered a stocking stuffed with gold coins and notes hidden beneath the floorboards.

Workmen digging a trench on a housing estate at Darfield, Yorkshire, in 1948 found an urn containing 500 Roman silver coins. The location of the find was only 200 yards from where a similar pot of coins was dug up twelve months earlier.

Two builders carrying out plumbing repairs in a house at Bootham, York, in 1953 found a bronze pot blocking one of the drains. When they managed to free it they were delighted to find that it contained 900 coins of Edward the First.

In the same year a group of Bradford schoolchildren playing in a derelict cottage, which had stood empty for almost thirty years, found 430 sovereigns and half-sovereigns together with £20 in silver coins. The money was in several small bags, each hidden in a different part of the building.

A hoard of gold ornaments dating from the Middle Bronze Age was found in 1954 by a farmer at Llanwrthwl, North Wales. A similar hoard turned up the following year a few miles away.

Another farmer ploughing a field near Redcar, Yorkshire, in 1954 spotted a silver coin lying in one of the furrows. He carried out a thorough search of the field and picked up 1,187 coins dating from the sixteenth and seventeenth centuries.

What can be learned from these brief accounts of accidental success which will help you find a hoard by deliberate search? Firstly, it should be noted that all of these people made their finds quite close to home. The same is true of almost all the major detector finds made in the past two or three years. It is quite unnecessary to travel long distances to reach likely hoard hunting sites. There is a hoard buried within a few miles of your home and your chances of finding it are far greater than are your chances of finding a hoard buried or hidden a hundred miles away. The time you spend travelling to and from a distant site can be put to more profitable use if you confine your search to local areas.

The second important lesson to be learned from the above stories is that more than half of them refer to hoards found in houses. Not in stately homes, or castles, or Elizabethan manors, but in the homes of ordinary people who had no idea their houses held fortunes. If yours is not the first family to occupy your house ask yourself how much you know about the previous occupants. Did they die unexpectedly? Did they go to gaol? Did they disappear without trace? Were they regarded by neighbours as a little eccentric? And what about the family who lived there before the previous owners? If yours is a Victorian house several families have spent their lives within its walls. The older your home the more likely it is that someone buried or hid something of value there in the past. You may be sceptical; you may think you have looked everywhere; but remember the lady with her chimney-sweeping brush in Hull . . . and the man who pulled up his floorboards in Newcastle-under-Lyme.

The whereabouts of one of the three hoards mentioned above found in open ground was first indicated by the finding of a single coin. The other two were found close to the location of another hoard discovered earlier or at some consequent date. Time and again this pattern has been repeated over the years, especially when hoards of Roman coins are concerned. A certain field will produce single Roman coins every time it is ploughed until one day an observant tractor driver spots a broken pot sticking out of the ground. He checks it and finds the bulk of the hoard. On other sites a complete pot of bronze coins will turn up and a few months or even years later the same field will produce another pot of silver coins. It is no exaggeration to say that a similar sequence of events has taken place hundreds of times throughout the country. Any field which has produced one pot or a number of single Roman coins is most likely to hold more.

The fourth clue to success which can be gleaned from these brief stories is found in the report concerning the Bradford schoolchildren. The cottage in which they were playing had stood empty for almost thirty years. During those years it had been visited by many adults—tramps, firewood hunters, local council officials, and others. Yet it took the bright and observant eyes of children to spot the hidden wealth. Therein lies the most important clue to success: unless you can look at any potential treasure site with the

Fig. 39 Thousands of nineteenth-century houses are demolished in Britain every year, and numerous hoards have been found by demolition contractors on sites such as this.

inquisitive, observant, and questioning eyes of a child you may miss the hoard which awaits you.

I advise town dwellers who hope to find a hoard to concentrate their research on houses. If your house has had more than one owner it is an excellent place to start your hunt. Search from top to bottom. Open the loft and check rafters and beams for money boxes screwed to their sides; carry out a careful detector survey of walls, chimney breasts, fireplaces, and floors. Pipework in walls and nails in floorboards do not prevent a detector search because they will give regular signals when you pass the search head over them. You can trace a pipe-run across a wall or a floor very accurately with a detector; if you obtain an unusual signal— either extremely loud or in some part of a room where buried metal is not expected to be found—you should investigate further. Look out for obvious signs that structural alterations have been made—loose floorboards, fresh

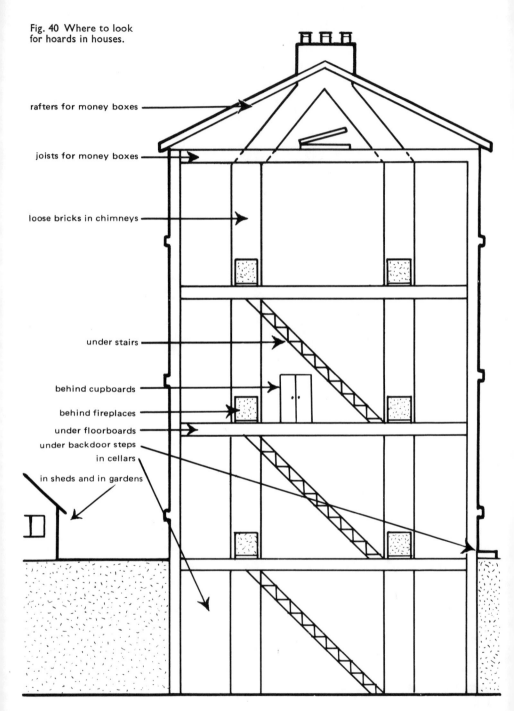

Fig. 40 Where to look for hoards in houses.

rafters for money boxes

joists for money boxes

loose bricks in chimneys

under stairs

behind cupboards

behind fireplaces

under floorboards

under backdoor steps

in cellars

in sheds and in gardens

84

mortar in brickwork, unusually thick walls, cupboards which appear too narrow—anything which might indicate that a previous owner had something to hide. Do not neglect cellars, outhouses, and gardens. Lawns and flower-beds have held pleasant surprises and there has often turned out to be more in an old shed than first meets the eye.

If your own house fails to hold a hoard do not despair. The experience you gain by searching it thoroughly will prove extremely useful later. Your next step should be to find out as much as possible about the people who have lived in your neighbourhood during the past fifty or so years. Older neighbours are mines of information. Talk to them as often as you can; soak up every drop of gossip, slander, and speculation. Find out where the eccentrics lived, where the sudden deaths occurred, where anyone with a colourful or a criminal background settled down. Soon you will build a picture of life in your district from the turn of the century to the present day. Check and, if possible, verify any story which interests you, by reading contemporary local newspapers, old electoral rolls, and any other written information your local library can provide.

When you feel you have sufficient evidence to indicate the possibility of hidden wealth in any house in your neighbourhood you must approach the present owner with the facts. Explain your interest in amateur treasure hunting; tell him of the research you have carried out which leads you to believe that something of value might be hidden on his property; explain that a search with a metal detector does not involve the demolition of half his house. You will almost certainly find that he is equally fascinated by the idea of a hoard in his home and permission for your search is most unlikely to be refused.

At this point I strongly advise that you draw up a *written* agreement with the owner of the house to share any find or any Treasure Trove reward which results from your search. Oral agreements are fine—until you find a sackful of sovereigns. With a written agreement you and the owner are committed to an arrangement made before you found anything of value. All you need are two pieces of paper

Fig. 41 Using a detector
to search a wall.

which read, 'We agree to share equally any find, Treasure
Trove reward, or other profit which results from a search
of . . . .'Add the address of the house and make sure you and
the owner date and sign both copies. You can then proceed
with the search which should be carried out in the same way
as you searched your own home.

Readers who live in the country should concentrate on
hunting a hoard buried in open ground. (It is worth noting
that there are many fascinating cottages and farmhouses in
country districts which might also repay attention.) Local
farmworkers are always very knowledgeable about fields
which have produced single coins when ploughed in the
past. Question them carefully and try to discover if the
coins are available for inspection. Some may have been
passed to local museums; others may still be in the posses-

Plate 5 These coins and tokens were recovered from the tidal foreshores of the Thames. Similar finds await amateur treasure hunters on all tidal rivers.

Plate 6 Rockhounds can find beautiful specimens like these in the mountainous regions of Britain. Examples shown are fluorite, pyrites and malachite.

Plate 7 Most amateur treasure hunting sites hold a wide assortment of lost buttons. These examples were all found on public footpaths.

Plate 8 Bottles recovered from Victorian dumps. The heavily embossed Warner's 'Safe' Cure, the blue and green ink and the intriguing marble-stoppered Cod are typical of late nineteenth century bottle-making craftsmanship.

sion of the people who found them. If you are able to examine them you should compare dates and the condition of each coin. Closely dated coins and any which appear to be in good condition are more likely to have come from a hoard than are coins of widely different dates or those which are very badly worn.

A single coin find is insufficient evidence to warrant a detector search of a large field. Several coins, especially if they are all closely dated and in good condition, are a better proposition. Find out more about the circumstances under which they were found. Establish the time of year, the depth at which the plough was set, and, most important of all, whether or not a hoard has already been found in the same field or somewhere nearby. If another hoard has turned up and the coins in it were of a different metal to the single ones we have been discussing the chances of a second hoard are very high.

If the coins are medieval or earlier you should at this point approach the local Archaeological Society in order to establish whether or not the field covers a known archaeological site. The Society's address is obtainable at your local library. Take a large-scale Ordnance Survey map of the area with you when you visit the Secretary of the Society and compare it with his map which shows the location of any archaeological site he suggests might lie under the field. If the field does indeed lie *directly* over the site I advise you to abandon the search unless the Secretary invites you to survey the site for the Society, in which case you will have to agree to search under supervision and to hand over all finds made to the Society.

If the coins are post-medieval or if there is no known archaeological site beneath the field you may now proceed to obtain the permission of the farmer to carry out the search. Again, it is important that you both sign copies of a written agreement to share any profit resulting from your search.

With permission obtained and an agreement signed you are ready to start your hunt. If there is a hoard of coins in the field it will be at least two feet down and possibly even

87

deeper. You could easily miss it by using the wrong metal detector. Forget about coinshooting—unless the single coins found are of exceptional interest or value—and use a unit with a large search coil. This will not find the single coins but it will certainly find the hoard if you use it correctly. A methodical lines and pins search is essential when hunting a hoard in an open field. You might have spent weeks or even months on research; to miss the hoard now because you used a random search pattern would be foolish. Do not concentrate the search on those spots which produced the single coins; ploughing can scatter coins over a wide area. Cover the entire site and even if you find nothing you will complete the search knowing that this particular field does not hold a hoard.

Never expect immediate success when hoard hunting. A lucky few may stumble across a spectacular find within a few hours of starting a search, but the majority will spend months or even years tracking down the hidden treasure they are seeking. Do not become obsessed by the idea of making a big find. Spend a few days each month on the project and do not neglect the other branches of the hobby by concentrating all of your efforts on hoard hunting. The treasure hunter who spends one year coinshooting often ends up with more valuable finds than the treasure hunter who spends three hundred and sixty-five days looking for the big one.

6 Treasure hunting problems

There is no doubt that substantial rewards await those electronics experts and inventors who can solve the problems which at present prevent treasure hunters finding more of the wealth which lies hidden under the ground, in houses, along riverbanks, on beaches, and beneath the sea. A metal detector sensitive *only* to gold, silver, copper and bronze is high on the list of developments eagerly awaited by professional treasure hunters who could put such a unit to highly profitable use. There are, however, a number of other problems in treasure hunting which cry out for a practical solution which would enable professionals *and* amateurs to find more.

We have already seen that beaches overlie a king's ransom in coins and jewellery which rests on the hard-pack. If a machine could be developed which would dig and turn the sand in the way a stormy sea does the job, and at the same time extract the valuable finds, there would be a long queue of treasure hunters waiting to buy. In the United States a beach cleaning machine has been developed by mechanical engineers to remove broken glass, tin cans and bottle tops from holiday beaches. It consists of a large

Fig. 42 Beach cleaning machine principles.

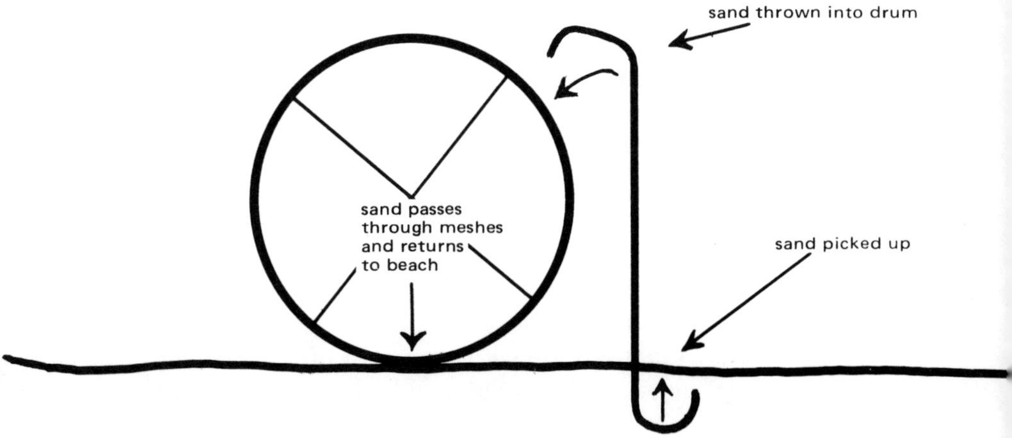

sand thrown into drum

sand passes through meshes and returns to beach

sand picked up

revolving drum which contains several wire-mesh screens. A power-driven shovel digs the beach immediately in front of the drum and passes it through the screens where refuse is removed before the sand is returned to the beach. With modifications to enable the shovel to dig deeper and with smaller screens capable of trapping coins and jewellery such a machine might solve the problem of finding more of the fortune on our beaches.

A tool which would enable newcomers to extract finds from the ground as neatly as professionals do the job would be a welcome innovation. A perfectly satisfactory job *can* be done with a sharp knife and a screwdriver blade, but there will always be a few irresponsible fools who dig unsightly holes and do not make a good job of filling them in again. Those of us who are interested in the growth of the hobby as a popular pastime would like to see the development of a small tool which even irresponsible fools could not use incorrectly.

Inexpensive underwater detectors would find a ready market in sub-aqua circles where the current price of several hundred pounds for a detector which can be operated by one man at depths of thirty feet or more is so high that such units can only be bought by clubs. Indications are that this problem might be solved shortly; several detector manufacturers have been working on inexpensive underwater models for some time and the race to be first on the market with a really low-cost unit is hotting up. When it appears there is no doubt that the number of finds made just beyond the breaking waves on beaches will increase dramatically.

Rivers and riversides have interested me for a number of years. The Thames, the Severn, and other major tidal rivers hold a wide assortment of exciting finds and those I have recovered so far convince me that developments in equipment for use in rivers are urgently needed. One has only to glimpse a few square inches of tidal riverbed through a glass-bottomed bucket to realize the potential for equipment which would hold back the water so that areas of bed normally covered at low tide could be thoroughly searched

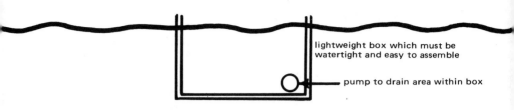

lightweight box which must be
watertight and easy to assemble

pump to drain area within box

Fig. 43 Searching below
low water mark.

by digging, sieving, and other methods. I have in mind a
watertight box, caisson, or cofferdam which could be
placed in the water at low tide. It would keep several
square yards of the bed dry for an hour or two while a
search was made before moving to a new site. I have tried a
few small experiments along these lines with wooden
boards and there is no doubt that the principle is sound.

Miniature suction dredges which can be operated by one
or two men are already with us. They were developed
several years ago in the United States and they have been
used with great success by gold prospectors seeking alluvial
gold in the streams and rivers of gold-bearing regions
throughout the world. In 1971 I used one of these machines
with fellow treasure hunter John Webb on the tidal reaches
of the Thames. We were both very interested to find out if
the principle of trapping gold dust and small nuggets on the
riffle boards could be applied to hunting coins and jewellery
in rivers. John also had plans to use the dredge on a gold-
hunting expedition in Scotland and I could see the machine's
potential for hunting semi-precious stones and freshwater
pearl mussels. The dredge consists of an open metal box
four feet long and eighteen inches wide which floats on two
large tyre inner tubes. The bottom of the box is covered by
riffle boards spaced at approximately three-inch intervals
which look rather like an old-fashioned washboard. At one
end of the box there is a metal cover and beneath this a
connection for a long hose which reaches down to the
riverbed. Behind the box a motor-driven pump is mounted
and connected to the suction hose in such a way that when

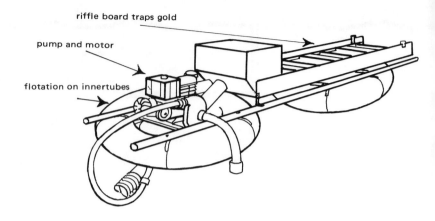

riffle board traps gold

pump and motor

flotation on innertubes

Fig. 44 A suction dredge.

the motor is running mud, sand and pebbles are drawn from the riverbed and washed across the riffles. Particles of gold, being exceptionally heavy, are trapped behind the riffles from where they can be collected when the motor is stopped.

John and I wanted to use the dredge in fairly shallow water so we reduced the length of the suction hose to fifteen feet. It was originally thirty feet long and the unit could, its manufacturer claimed, pick up a gold nugget at that depth and deposit it on the riffles with no trouble at all. He could not tell us if the riffles would also trap silver and copper coins so it was a question of paying our money and taking our chances.

We were pleasantly surprised. Within two minutes of starting the motor we saw a Victorian ring trapped in the riffles and we went on to find a number of coins, buttons, and other interesting finds on that first run. Unfortunately there were a number of problems which, even now, have not been overcome. Large stones, clay, plastic bags, and similar junk which litters the bed of the Thames (and other rivers) quickly block the suction hose. Gold is easily trapped by the riffles but some small and lightweight silver, copper, and bronze objects are carried across and can be lost unless a sieve or some other trap is fitted at the end of the machine. The unit is also very heavy and difficult to get down to the water's edge on rivers in towns and cities. Nevertheless, we have proved its potential. With some modifications it could become a first-class treasure hunting tool.

The above are just a few of the ideas on treasure hunting equipment which have crossed my mind during the past year or so. No doubt you will soon have your own suggestions for improving or modifying the tools you use. If you can match those suggestions with electronic or engineering skills I urge you to put them to the test. Amateur treasure hunting is still a young hobby and there are many unexplored avenues for enthusiasts with inventive minds.

7 Bottles, pipes and pot lids

Readers as yet uninitiated into the fascinating world of bottle collecting may be surprised to learn that Victorian rubbish dumps hold rich prizes for those prepared to undertake the necessary research to pinpoint a dump's location and the hard digging involved in the recovery of bottles. Thousands of superb examples of nineteenth-century bottle-making craftsmanship have been dug out of the ground by members of the British Bottle Collectors Club and this branch of amateur treasure hunting has in recent years become immensely popular. The magazine *Bottles and Relics News* reports every month on British finds and a glance through half a dozen back copies reveals the wealth of colourful and collectable bottles, pipes, pot lids, dolls' heads, and other fascinating objects which have so far been recovered from long-forgotten dumps.

The methods of locating and digging Victorian dumps are thoroughly covered in my earlier book, *Bottle Collecting*. Since the book's publication thousands of men, women, and children who previously regarded the collecting of Victoriana as a costly hobby have found to their delight that it is possible to build up a valuable collection of pre-1900 specimens for little more than the cost of a digging fork. A number of schools have started their own bottle museums after successful group digs and the objects found on such expeditions have led to greater interest in local history, early advertising, and similar informative and educational subjects. There has also been a rapid growth in the number of bottle shops catering to the needs of collectors who do not wish to indulge in the rather strenuous work of bottle recovery. An incredible variety of dump finds are on sale and it is the growth of these retail outlets which has provided a profitable market for diggers interested in selling large quantities of bottles.

I said in *Bottle Collecting* that glass-marble stoppered bottles and transfer-marked stoneware ginger beers were likely to be the most sought-after varieties when interest in the hobby became widespread. This has proved to be an

Fig. 45 Members of the British Bottle Collectors Club on a club 'dig'. The site is a Victorian rubbish dump.

Fig. 46 A Hamilton bottle recovered by a happy digger.

accurate forecast, but I am delighted to find that interest in other bottles has also grown. Cobalt blue poisons, sheared lip inks, and embossed beers have proved immensely popular and many collectors have already begun to specialize in these varieties. One specialized interest which I did not cover in *Bottle Collecting* but which has proved very popular is the collecting of bottle stoppers. I have seen some fine collections of these previously disregarded dump finds which are best displayed by embedding them in plaster to make plaques which can be mounted on walls. Impressive stopper collections can be built up very quickly because even though a bottle may break when it is thrown into a dump the stopper remains intact.

The varieties of clay tobacco pipes which have come out of the ground in the past two years are quite remarkable. All over Britain hitherto unrecorded specimens of these delightful nineteenth-century relics have been found. It seems that Victorian pipe makers recorded every major event, every politician, every music-hall celebrity, and every military hero on the pipe bowls they designed between 1870 and 1900. My most interesting find so far this year is a pipe found in Essex which depicts the generals Kruger and Buller. Others reported by British Bottle Collectors Club members include a bowl recording the first parachute jump, a bowl in the shape of the head of Ally Sloper, who was a famous Victorian cartoon character, and a bowl in the shape of an elephant's head. Several hundred similar finds of new varieties have been made and interest in clay tobacco pipe collecting continues to grow.

It was obvious to most people digging Victorian dumps two or three years ago that pot lids would soon become the most sought-after relics. The collecting of coloured varieties was already popular before Queen Victoria died and interest in them has pushed prices far out of reach for those whose collecting budget is strictly limited. Fortunately a few coloured specimens did find their way into rubbish dumps and one or two lucky diggers have recovered coloured pot lids worth many pounds. But it is the more common black and white varieties which have attracted

Fig. 47 Pipes found in rubbish dumps.

97

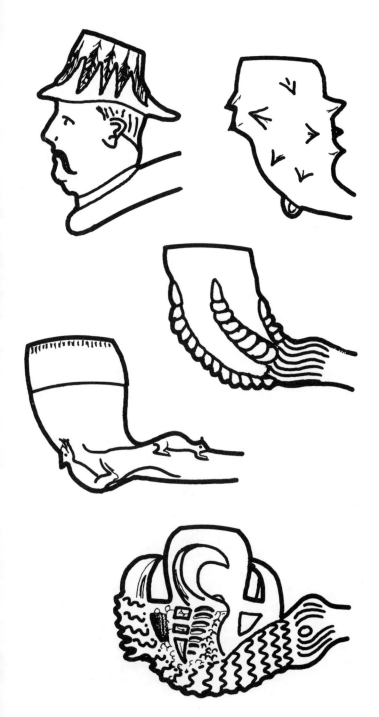

most attention among dump diggers recently. They are by no means easy to find; only early dumps hold sufficient quantities for experienced diggers to recover one or two during a full day of hard digging. Nevertheless, impressive collections have been built up by those who have found the right dumps. One member of the British Bottle Collectors Club has a collection of more than two hundred—all of which came from the same dump; and over seven hundred different varieties have been recorded by diggers throughout Britain. I estimate that figure will approach four thousand when dumps in more remote regions are located and dug. Demand for these extremely interesting examples of Victorian advertising has far outstripped supplies and prices are rising rapidly. Fortunately sufficient numbers await recovery to make it possible for anyone determined to find them to build a collection by diligent digging.

Fig. 48 Two attractive Victorian pot lids recovered from an old dump.

Keeping pace with this rapid growth of interest in the finding and collecting of bottles, pipes, and pot lids has been a growing demand for information on bottle works, breweries, mineral water companies, wine merchants, pipe makers, quack medicine vendors, and the manufacturers of tooth powders, meat and fish pastes, mustards, grate blacking, and all the other products which were sold in the nineteenth century. It is their containers which make up the contents of all Victorian rubbish dumps and today's collectors are eager to learn as much about them as possible. The recording of finds made by members of the British Bottle Collectors Club has helped enormously in establishing the distribution and rarity of many dump finds; but it is the number of experts who have written informative articles for *Bottles and Relics News* on their specialized interests which has enabled so much useful information to be passed on to Britain's growing fraternity of bottle collectors. I hope that they and many other authorities will continue to share their knowledge with all of us who are so fascinated by this subject.

8 Rockhounding

Every ounce of gold and silver which has been stored in the world's bank vaults or used to make coins and jewellery was originally found in a mine or in a river; every precious gem in the Crown Jewels originally came out of the ground; and every metal object you locate with your detector was originally dug up as a metal ore. Unfortunately the vast deposits of precious metals and gems which provided the raw materials for the Crown Jewels and for the gold bars in the Bank of England are not to be found in Britain. We must content ourselves with less spectacular natural resources—though it is worth noting that a goldmine in Merionethshire was re-opened to obtain sufficient gold to make the wedding ring of Queen Elizabeth II, and that a sizeable diamond was found about one hundred years ago in a stream in County Fermanagh.

An astonishing variety of precious gems and minerals *can* be found in Britain but very few are obtainable in commercial quantities nowadays. Things were rather different in the past. There was a goldrush in Sutherland in the nineteenth century and large quantities of gold were also panned from the burns around Wanlockhead and Leadhills in the Southern Uplands of Scotland from the twelfth century until quite recent times. Every schoolboy knows that the Romans mined gold in Wales but it is not generally known that Ireland supplied large amounts of gold to the Roman Empire. Many geologists believe that even larger deposits of gold still await discovery deep beneath Ireland's Wicklow Hills. Silver and freshwater pearls were also exploited in Britain by the Romans. The silver came mainly from Cornwall, the Mendips, and the Pennines while pearl mussels could be found in many rivers in the south-west of England, parts of northern England, and most of Scotland and Ireland. Tin, copper, and lead were also mined in these and other regions on a fairly large scale until the end of the nineteenth century.

Today the mines are idle; the commercial deposits of ore long ago exhausted; the machinery and buildings overgrown with weeds; the bonanzas of yesteryear merely flickering memories. But the spirit which drove the old miners to seek the riches of the earth lives on. On summer weekends the mountains and moors of these former mining regions draw Britain's rockhounds as a magnet draws pins. Equipped with rock hammers, picks, geological maps, gold pans, and haversacks they scour the old mine workings, quarries, streams, and rocky outcrops for the smaller ore veins which the miners left untouched. They find gold, silver, copper, tin, and lead ores; they carry home delightful crystal specimens of semi-precious gems—amethyst, cornelian, agate, cairngorm, rose quartz, and many more. Some of the specimens are left in their natural state to be displayed in collecting cabinets; others are cut and polished in home gem-cutting workshops to make attractive jewellery and ornaments. Nobody gets rich but everybody gets an enormous amount of pleasure from the scenery, the great outdoors, and the small finds which are made.

My earlier book, *Rock and Gem Polishing*, contains detailed information on how and where to hunt semi-precious gems in Britain. I recommend this branch of the hobby to all amateur treasure hunters whether or not they wish to cut and polish the stones which they find. There are other exciting discoveries to be made around the old mines—bottle dumps, mining relics, lost coins, even possible hoards.

Readers interested in freshwater pearls will find the glass-bottomed bucket used to search riverbeds for lost coins and jewellery an ideal tool for hunting the large, black pearl mussels which can still be found in some rivers and streams of northern and western Britain. Return to the water any you find which are less than four inches long and which do not have ridged markings on the outer shell which indicate that a pearl has formed inside. To open smaller mussels and those which do not have these markings is wasteful and unprofitable. Put them back into the water and they may grow a pearl in the future.

Prospecting for gold by panning the gravels and sand of mountain streams in Britain's former gold mining regions is great fun. You will never get rich at the job but with patience and endeavour you could find a few flakes of raw British gold. A deft touch is needed with the pan and I advise you to practice at home before you head for the hills. Mix three or four ounces of small lead shot with several pounds of sand and gravel. Place a spadeful of this mixture in your pan and fill up with water at the kitchen sink. You must now swirl and tip the pan repeatedly to wash the lighter material over the sides until only the heavier lead shot is left. When you can do this without losing a single piece of lead you are ready to try your hand at the real thing.

The most favourable site for a deposit of alluvial gold is in the slack water of an active stream along its middle reaches, especially where it surges out of a mountain valley onto a flat area. Here it must drop its treasure as it loses the power to carry heavier objects. Find such a stream in an area where gold was once mined and you may experience the thrill which made the hearts of the Californian Forty-Niners and the men of the Klondike beat so fast. The flakes of gold you find in an auriferous stream are known as 'colour'. Follow the colour upstream, trying first one tributary then another. As the amount of colour increases and the tiny flakes in your pan become gradually larger you are nearing the original source of the gold. If the colour suddenly ceases to show you have passed the point where the original vein supplied the stream and you must retrace your steps and work the gravels and sand below this point. The suction dredge mentioned in chapter 6 would be useful on such a site.

9 Rules and regulations

The most important rules for all amateur treasure hunters are those laid down in the Code of Conduct. They are so important that I shall repeat them once again and ask anyone who has not yet done so to memorize them now.

1. Don't interfere with archaeological sites or ancient monuments. Join your local archaeological society if you are interested in ancient history.

2. Don't leave a mess. It is perfectly simple to extract a coin or other small object buried a few inches under the ground without digging a great hole. Use a sharpened trowel or a knife to cut a neat circle; extract the object; replace the soil and grass carefully and even *you* will have difficulty in finding the spot again.

3. Help keep Britain tidy—and help yourself. Bottle tops, silver paper, and tin cans are the last things you should throw away. You could well be digging them up again next year. So do yourself and the community a favour by taking all rusty junk you find to the nearest litter bin.

4. Don't trespass. Ask permission before venturing onto any private land.

5. Report all unusual historical finds to your local museum and get expert help if you accidentally discover a site of archaeological interest.

6. Learn the Treasure Trove laws and report all finds of gold and silver objects to the police. You will be well rewarded if the objects you find are declared Treasure Trove.

7. Respect the Country Code. Don't leave gates open when crossing fields and don't damage crops or frighten animals.

8. Never miss an opportunity to show and explain your detector to anyone who asks about it. Be friendly. You could pick up some clues to a good site.

9. If you meet another detector user while out on a hunt introduce yourself. You could probably teach each other a lot.

10. Finally, remember that when you are out with your

detector you are an ambassador for the whole amateur treasure hunting fraternity. Don't give us a bad name.

Treasure Trove

The Treasure Trove laws are beneficial to all amateur treasure hunters. They protect your interests if you find objects of gold or silver and I urge you to seek their protection if and when you find such objects. They can be summarized as follows. If an amateur treasure hunter (or anyone else) finds a hoard of gold or silver coins or any other object made from these metals he must *immediately* report his find to the local Coroner through the police or a local museum. One of these bodies will take charge of the find and give the finder a receipt. A Coroner's inquest will later be held to decide whether or not the find is Treasure Trove. The Coroner must decide if the objects were hidden by the owner with the intention of recovery at a later date, and he must also decide who found the objects on which the inquest is being held.

For example, if you found a pot of ancient gold or silver coins buried in a field it is highly likely that the person who buried them intended to dig them up again at a later date had not death or some other agency intervened. In this case the Coroner would almost certainly declare the find to be Treasure Trove. It would immediately become the property of the Crown and you, as finder, would receive a reward equal to the *full current market value of the find*. If the objects were not required by a museum they would be returned to you in lieu of a reward or the British Museum would sell them on your behalf at the best possible price obtainable.

If the gold and silver objects were modern, exhaustive enquiries would be made by the police to trace the owner. If he was traced the objects would be returned to him and you would receive no reward—though the owner *might* give you a reward for your services. If the owner could not be traced and the Coroner declared the find Treasure Trove you would receive the full market value reward.

If you were working with another amateur hunter or with a group when you made the find the Coroner might decide the reward should be shared by all the finders unless the group had agreed beforehand that finds would not be shared, in which case the reward would go to the amateur treasure hunter who located and recovered the find.

If the Coroner decided that a find of gold or silver was *not* Treasure Trove because there was insufficient evidence to suggest that the object or objects were hidden with the intention of recovery the owner of the property on which the find was made would also have a claim to ownership. Such a situation might arise in the case of a single coin or other object which might have been lost, thrown away, or donated to a religious shrine (e.g. a sacred well). In these cases the original owner had no intention of recovering the object. If you were searching a piece of ground without the owner's permission and you found such a single gold or silver object, and if the owner of the land claimed the object at the inquest, it is very likely that the Coroner would order it to be given to him. It is, therefore, of the utmost importance that you obtain the owner's permission before searching the property. If you both sign an agreement to share the finds made or the rewards received for finding them you are certain of half the value of finds which are not Treasure Trove, while the owner of the land can be certain of a half share in any Treasure Trove find you make.

Archaeological finds Ancient coins and other antiquities made from copper, bronze, or any other base metal are not Treasure Trove and need not be reported to the local Coroner when found. Under Rule Five of the Code of Conduct such finds must be reported to your local museum. I also recommend that you donate them to the museum and that at the same time you write to the Secretary of the Council for British Archaeology informing him of your donation.

Modern finds As a successful amateur treasure hunter you can confidently expect to find approximately fifty objects during a full day spent coinshooting on public footpaths, riversides, and similar sites. Your day's haul might include thirty modern coins, fifteen Victorian coins, two gold rings, a cigarette lighter, a bunch of keys, and a purse containing several pound notes. It is your duty to give the owners of these objects every opportunity to claim them. You might do this in several ways. You might hand them in at your local police station; you might advertise in a local newspaper, or you might pin a notice to your garden gate or front door announcing you had found a certain object and that the owner should collect it from you. Common sense must guide you here. It would obviously waste your time and the time of the local police if you handed in every find you made or advertised every item you found. Objects such as purses and bunches of keys are best handed to the police because they are more likely to be claimed by their owners. After a period of time they will be returned to you to dispose of as you see fit, but you must always be prepared to surrender to its owner any object which the police return to you should the owner claim it at some time in the future. Nobody is likely to claim a purse containing Victorian coins or a bunch of keys rusty with age, but objects which have obviously been lost quite recently should never be disposed of until you have made every possible effort to trace their owners.

Most professional coinshooters, who find thousands of objects every year, operate the following simple system when dealing with modern finds. All purses, wallets, valuable modern jewellery, and bunches of keys are handed in at the local police station. If they are not claimed after a period of time they are redeemed and disposed of. If the owner turns up later his property is recovered and returned to him. Modern coins, inexpensive jewellery, and other finds of little value are not handed to the police, but the coinshooter ensures that local people know he owns a metal detector and that he searches local sites. If they lose a small object on one of these sites they know that they can visit the coinshooter's home with a very good chance of recovering the lost object. This system appears to work very well for those professionals of my acquaintance and I recommend it to you.

Gold prospecting Gold mining rights are vested in the Crown. Before you pan for gold in a mountain stream you must obtain the permission of the owner of the land and you must also obtain a Crown Estate Permit which costs £10 plus £1·28 office charges and stamp duty.

Wreck material Objects washed ashore from a wreck should be handed to the local Coastguard. If unclaimed they will be returned to you and you may have to pay a fee for storage.

Permission to search and to dig You have no right to search or to dig anywhere other than on property which you own. Permission from the owner must always be obtained before you carry out any amateur treasure hunting activity on private land. Searches on beaches, riversides, and similar sites can usually be undertaken without first seeking permission but if you are ordered to stop you must do so at once. Rubbish dumps and disused mines are all owned by someone and it is your duty to ask permission before you dig on them. A polite request is most unlikely to be refused.

10 Useful addresses

When writing to any of the addresses listed below to obtain leaflets, catalogues, or information you must enclose a stamped addressed envelope if you require a prompt reply.

The British Amateur Treasure Hunting Club, Greenacres, Church Road, Black Notley, Braintree, Essex.

The club organizes local activities through its County Secretaries who arrange treasure hunts, discussions, and research activities for local members. A full list of County Secretaries can be obtained from the London headquarters address. Membership fee: £1·50 per year; children 50p.

The British Bottle Collectors Club, Greenacres, Church Road, Black Notley, Braintree, Essex.

The club compiles information on the bottles, pipes, pot lids, and other dump finds made by members. Other membership benefits include contacts with other local members, club digs, and affiliated membership of overseas bottle collecting clubs. Membership fee: £1·00 per year; children 50p.

True Treasure Monthly, Greenacres, Church Road, Black Notley, Braintree, Essex.

A monthly magazine for all interested in treasure hunting. Contains amateur treasure hunting site reports, treasure stories, and news from the world of treasure hunting. Single copies 15p. Yearly subscription £1·95 including postage.

Bottles and Relics News (incorporating Rockhound), Greenacres, Church Road, Black Notley, Braintree, Essex.

A monthly magazine for all bottle collectors. Contains authoritative articles on bottle history, pot lids, clay tobacco pipes, and other dump finds. Single copies 15p. Yearly subscription £1·95 including postage.

Metal detector retailers:
Joan Allen Electronics Ltd
    184 Main Road, Biggin Hill, Kent.
    35 Craven Street, London W.C.2.
    9 High Street, Totnes, South Devon.

Treasure Hunting Supplies
    71 Caledonian Road, London N.1.
    175 Church Road, Willesden, London N.W.10.
    68 Gillygate, York.
    139 Witton Street, Northwich, Cheshire.
M. L. Beach (Products) Ltd
    41 Church Street, Twickenham, Middlesex.
    7 Kings Parade, Ditchling Road, Brighton.
Midas Instruments Ltd
    26 Cottam Crescent, Marple Bridge, Cheshire.
C-Scope Metal Detectors
    62 Castle Street, Canterbury, Kent.
Underground Exploration
    Faraday House, P.O. Box 1, Hailsham, Sussex.
Pulse Induction Ltd
    Greencoat House, Francis Street, London S.W.1.

Index

amateur archaeologists 55
archaeological
    finds 107
    societies 87
armchairs 6

back doors 9
barges 16
beaches 67
Bedford 18
bedrooms 13
Boston 16
bottles 94
Bottles and Relics News 110
bridges 15, 17, 19, 24, 31
Bristol 16
British Amateur Treasure Hunting Club 110
British Bottle Collectors Club 110

Cambridge 18
canals 18
children 12
clay tobacco pipes 19, 96
Code of Conduct 54, 105
coin
    losses 6
    Roman 82
    traps 33, 46
coinshooting 40
currents 72

detectors
    BFO 43
    depth penetration 45
    IB 47
    Pulse induction 48, 69
    retailers 110
    T/R 45
    underwater 90
    waterproof 51
dredges 91

eddy currents 24

ferries 17

floating sieves 23, 35
flood prevention 19
footpaths 56
fords 15, 17, 38
front doors 9

gales 74
gas meters 11
glass-bottomed buckets 20
gold 15, 28, 102
    panning 103
    prospecting 109
grass
    slopes 63
    verges 60
Grove Wood Treasure 41

hard-pack 69
headphones 50
Hertford 18
hoards 40, 79
houses 81
    searches 83
Hull 16
human behaviour 11

Ipswich 16

jewellery 65

lead tallies 15
lines and pins 65
locks 12
London 16
Longshore Drift 72
Lynn 16

mantelshelves 11
Mersey 19
meters 50
modern finds 107

nail clusters 34

Newcastle-upon-Tyne 16
Nottingham 18

open spaces 62
Ordnance Survey maps 56
Ouse 16

patience 13
pearls 102
permission 87, 109
Peterborough 18
ports 16
pot lids 96

recording finds 37
research 20, 66
river rakes 20
rivers
    history 14
    meanders 38
    movement 26
    non-tidal 24
    tidal 30
    weight distribution 28
roads 17
rockhounding 102

safety 24

sand sifting 67
search coils 50
search techniques 57
secluded spots 65
Severn 16, 18
shingle patches 74
Shrewsbury 18
silver 102
skirting boards 8
Southampton 16, 19
Stratford-on-Avon 18

Thames 18
tides 37, 71
    tables 31
tokens 15
Treasure Trove 106
trees 63
Trent 16
True Treasure Monthly 110
tuners 51

wharves 15
wreck material 109
wrecks 76
Wye 18

Yarmouth 16